IT HAPPENED TO ME

Series Editor: Arlene Hirschfelder

Books in the It Happened to Me series are designed for inquisitive teens digging for answers about certain illnesses, social issues, or lifestyle interests. Whether you are deep into your teen years or just entering them, these books are gold mines of up-to-date information, riveting teen views, and great visuals to help you figure out stuff. Besides special boxes highlighting singular facts, each book is enhanced with the latest reading list, websites, and an index. Perfect for browsing, there's loads of expert information by acclaimed writers to help parents, guardians, and librarians understand teen illness, tough situations, and lifestyle choices.

1. *Learning Disabilities: The Ultimate Teen Guide,* by Penny Hutchins Paquette and Cheryl Gerson Tuttle, 2003.
2. *Epilepsy: The Ultimate Teen Guide,* by Kathlyn Gay and Sean McGarrahan, 2002.
3. *Stress Relief: The Ultimate Teen Guide,* by Mark Powell, 2002.
4. *Making Sexual Decisions: The Ultimate Teen Guide*, by L. Kris Gowen, Ph.D., 2003.
5. *Asthma: The Ultimate Teen Guide,* by Penny Hutchins Paquette, 2003.
6. *Cultural Diversity: Conflicts and Challenges: The Ultimate Teen Guide,* by Kathlyn Gay, 2003.
7. *Diabetes: The Ultimate Teen Guide,* by Katherine J. Moran, 2004.
8. *When Will I Stop Hurting? Teens, Loss, and Grief: The Ultimate Teen Guide,* by Edward Myers, 2004.
9. *Volunteering: The Ultimate Teen Guide*, by Kathlyn Gay, 2004.
10. *Organ Transplants: A Survival Guide for the Entire Family: The Ultimate Teen Guide,* by Tina P. Schwartz, 2005.
11. *Medications: The Ultimate Teen Guide*, by Cheryl Gerson Tuttle, 2005.

Self-Advocacy

The Ultimate Teen Guide

CHERYL GERSON TUTTLE
JOANN AUGERI SILVA

It Happened to Me, No. 19

The Scarecrow Press, Inc.
Lanham, Maryland • Toronto • Plymouth, UK
2007

SCARECROW PRESS, INC.

Published in the United States of America
by Scarecrow Press, Inc.
A wholly owned subsidiary of The Rowman & Littlefield Publishing Group, Inc.
4501 Forbes Boulevard, Suite 200, Lanham, Maryland 20706
www.scarecrowpress.com

Estover Road
Plymouth PL6 7PY
United Kingdom

British Library Cataloguing in Publication Information Available

Library of Congress Cataloging-in-Publication Data

Tuttle, Cheryl Gerson.
  Self-advocacy : the ultimate teen guide / Cheryl Gerson Tuttle, JoAnn Augeri Silva.
   p. cm. — (It happened to me ; no. 19)
  Includes bibliographical references and index.
  ISBN-13: 978-0-8108-5646-2 (hardcover : alk. paper)
  ISBN-10: 0-8108-5646-8 (hardcover : alk. paper)
  1. Children's rights—United States. 2. Youth—Legal status, laws, etc.—United States.
  3. Teenagers—United States—Life skills guides. 4. Self-help techniques—United States.
  I. Silva, JoAnn Augeri, 1944– II. Title.
  HV741.T88 2007
  646.700835—dc22

                       2007002221

⊚™ The paper used in this publication meets the minimum requirements of
American National Standard for Information Sciences—Permanence of Paper
for Printed Library Materials, ANSI/NISO Z39.48-1992.
Manufactured in the United States of America.

For Penny Paquette, who kept me going.—CGT
For Anthony.—JAS

Contents

Acknowledgments

We gratefully acknowledge the assistance, cooperation, and encouragement of the following people, without whom this book would not have been possible: Paul Tremblay, Professor, Boston College Law School; Marianne Murphy; Casey Family Services staff, Lowell, Mass.; R. Anthony Silva; Rachel Rowe Ausband; Bill Ausband; attorney Stacey Violante Cote, University of Connecticut School of Law Teen Advocacy Center; attorney Barbara Kaban, Children's Law Center of Massachusetts; attorney Rebecca Vose, JRAP; Penny Hutchins Paquette; the Unitarian Universalist Association of Congregations Our Whole Lives Program; Meghan Parsons; Stefan Russo, Goddard Riverside Community Center; Vincent Verrassi, metropolitan campus director of the regional center at Fairleigh Dickinson University; Daphne Gregory, transition coordinator at Milburn High School, Milburn, N.J.; Lilliam Barrios-Paoli, David Rubin, Jeff Sobel, Alexandria Sumpter-Delves, Claudia Molina, Cassildra Aguilera, and Leslie Blumgold from Safe Space; Keith Hefner, Youth Connections; Ray Pultinas, DeWitt Clinton High School; and Henry Frommer.

We would also like to thank the young people who were willing to share their stories to encourage other teens to advocate for themselves. Finally, we want to thank our family and friends for their continued support and patience.

Introduction

Why would we write a book on self-advocacy for teens?

- ◉ **To recognize that young people your age face many obstacles and that you can't always depend on the adults around you to fight your battles.**
- ◉ **To show that you do not need to be a victim when you are faced with situations that are unfair, immoral, illegal, and unjust.**
- ◉ **To let you know that you can speak up for yourself.**
- ◉ **To help teens like you who want to improve their own lives and the lives of others.**
- ◉ **To give you the tools to succeed when you decide to challenge the status quo.**

For all of these reasons and more, we've put together a book we hope you will find full of information and resources.

For most of you, school is the most time-consuming and important part of your life. Your school principal expects you to show up every day, to obey school rules, and not to cause trouble. In class, teachers expect you to pay attention and to learn the subjects they teach. School administrators expect you to pass the courses you take and to pass the standardized tests more and more states require before students can graduate from high school. Living a successful life, however, will depend not only on what you learn in your classrooms but also on what you learn about yourself. Your teen years will shape you in more than academic ways. What you encounter and what you might have to overcome in school and in your activities out of school will help you prepare for independence—that is, the rest of your life.

Like many teens, you may depend on your parents to be your advocates. They meet with teachers at conference time to make sure you are getting the education you need. If you receive special education services, they attend meetings and work with your teachers to develop your educational plan and discuss your academic plans after high school. They meet with your doctors to make sure that your medical care is appropriate. They might talk with their friends and business associates to try to get you a good summer job. When you have a problem, they help make sure that your rights are upheld. In return, they expect you to take your schooling seriously and to do the best you can.

Some of you already have had to take on the responsibilities we mention because you have lost one or both parents or because you are in foster care. If you are reading this book, you already may have experienced some form of discrimination or injustice that you want to resolve. If so, now is the time to determine how to take over some "adult" responsibilities in an effective, meaningful way.

The best way to learn to be independent is to find out how to take care of yourself. If you don't already, you will need to master the basics: how to manage your money, how to shop, how to cook, how to do laundry, and how to do many other things that will help you be successful and independent. However, taking care of yourself involves much more than knowing how to do everyday things. Taking care of yourself means standing up for yourself and making sure you get what you need and are entitled to in life. That's what this book can help you do. In the first three chapters, we explain what self-advocacy is step by step and why it might be necessary to speak up for yourself, how to go about self-advocating successfully, and how to wisely use the power of the media if you publicize your cause.

Then, we devote seven individual chapters to some issues you face as a teen that might require you to advocate for yourself: learning disabilities, physical disabilities, school issues, personal rights, sexuality, legal issues, and foster care. You may choose to read the whole book or choose to read just the first three chapters and the issue-related chapter that applies to your situation.

We encourage you to read on, to find out how learning to self-advocate can help you offset and counter the obstacles you face, and how you can make your life safer, more satisfying, and more rewarding.

Why You Should Be Your Own Advocate

Do you know what it means to be an advocate? According to one dictionary, *advocacy* is "the act or process of advocating or supporting a cause or proposal." Another dictionary defines *advocate* as someone who "speaks out for a cause and works toward a solution." When you are an advocate for yourself, you plead for and support yourself and your needs. You also work toward a solution for whatever problem you are facing. Because you know best what your needs are, you are the best person to do this. When you advocate for yourself, you are affecting the decisions that become part of your daily life. You might ask, "How can I make myself heard? How can I bring about solutions to problems? Why do I need to plead for or support myself in the first place?"

The United States was founded on the principle of equality and fundamental rights. For the most part, government agencies and other institutions function efficiently. Everyone, including young people, has the basic rights promised by the Declaration of Independence: "Life, Liberty and the Pursuit of Happiness." Things can go wrong, though. You probably know of many such incidents. Perhaps a friend was suspended from school for something he or she absolutely did not do. Perhaps you yourself have been unjustly accused of doing something against the rules. Perhaps you have had experiences in which you felt you were treated unfairly and that your rights were being violated.

In cases you may have heard of, young people have objected to the rules most of us follow every day. You may have read about the student who objected to reciting the pledge of allegiance in school because the pledge includes the words *under God*. You may have studied about the U.S. Supreme Court case *Brown v. Board of Education* (1954) that did away with racial segregation in the public schools. In each of these cases, someone spoke up against rules he or she disagreed with and thought were unfair. Someone pleaded a case and supported an idea, and that action changed minds, policies, and institutions. By speaking up and advocating for their beliefs, those people made a difference in the lives of many others.

There are many reasons you may need to advocate for yourself. When you live in a large society, you interact with many different people with many different opinions. You may have been, or are now, the victim of prejudice or negative attitudes. You may even have negative attitudes about other people. When you were younger, you might have thought "Girls are dumb and can't play sports," or "Boys are wild and I shouldn't play with them." As you got older and more experienced, you learned that people are more complicated. You have found out that many girls are great at sports, and many boys are sensitive and kind. If you learned this, you overcame the prejudices you had as a child, and your former prejudices did not harm anyone.

However, not everyone outgrows his or her prejudices. Sometimes, prejudices are part of a family's, a community's, or an entire region's deeply held beliefs. When that is the case, prejudice can lead to discrimination, which creates barriers that prevent people from participating fully in society. If a prejudice leads to discrimination against you and creates barriers for your full participation in society, you will need to advocate for yourself. When prejudice affects national issues, like racial segregation in public schools, many agencies work together, often with lawyers, to resolve those issues and change laws. When local issues need to be addressed—for example, special education accommodations, school discipline, even dress codes at school—one person can make a difference.

That person can be you. When something affects you personally, such as racial profiling, your involvement with the legal system, or your desire to live independently despite your physical disability, you need to speak up for yourself.

KNOW WHEN YOU CAN MAKE A DIFFERENCE

Self-advocacy is not something to be taken lightly. For example, if you feel a slight based on a simple misunderstanding or if you don't get the part you wanted in a school play, you will not need or want to speak up and work against the establishment. There are times when you know that your rights or the rights of others have been violated and you need to take a stand. This chapter and the rest of this book will help you know when those times are.

Here are ways to determine whether the situation you face calls for action:

- When you see that everyone else in your school, community, or religious institution is treated one way and you are treated a different way because of your race, gender, disability, or religion, it is time to consider self-advocacy.
- When you believe you need something special because of a disability, a medical condition, or a special life circumstance to succeed as other students do, it is time to consider self-advocacy.
- When you believe that your treatment in a particular situation is illegal, it is time to consider self-advocacy.
- When you find yourself in trouble or facing a difficult challenge in school, with the legal system, or in your personal life, it is time to consider self-advocacy.

Self-advocacy does not have to be confrontational or unpleasant. Self-advocacy involves knowing your strengths and needs, knowing your rights, identifying your goals, and being able to communicate all of this to others in a way and at a time that will make a difference. Not all incidents or issues need to be dealt with by writing or changing laws. In many cases, simply and firmly, but politely, reminding your employer, your teacher, your friend, or a ticket taker at the movies of your situation and your needs can be considered self-advocacy. When you do this, you are speaking up for yourself and asking for what you need. Self-advocacy does not have to mean that someone else will get less because you need more. Allowing students of all religions, races, and sexual orientations to participate in all activities does not diminish the participation of those students who consider themselves "normal." Installing a ramp in a theater or painting bright stripes on stairs to aid people with limited vision are not actions that make it harder for those who do not have limited mobility or vision problems.

SELF-ADVOCACY TAKES COURAGE

It takes a lot of courage to advocate for yourself. You have to speak up about what is bothering you. You have to talk, perhaps publicly, about what you are experiencing, and that can make you feel vulnerable and uncomfortable. You have to deal with the adults you are confronting or asking for help to come to a solution to your problem.

In September 2005, students at a New York high school did just that. The education department had installed metal detectors at the entrance of the school because of the area's high crime rate (see chapter 5). One student organized a protest through a website, and fifteen hundred students walked to the education department's office demanding to be heard. Their efforts effected a change; an idea that began with one student is having far-reaching results for the rest of the students at the school.

Confronting adults and speaking up for yourself and your group are not easy tasks, but taking them on is better than the alternative. If you become angry without speaking up to make things better, the unfair situation will remain the same and perhaps get even worse.

THE HISTORY OF SELF-ADVOCACY

Failing to act can have wide-ranging effects. During the 1960s, teenagers began to be taken seriously because they got involved in broader social issues and youth-related causes:

◎ **If you just get angry without self-advocacy or just remain quiet and accept what you perceive as an unjust situation, you miss out on all the possibilities that could take place if the problem were solved in a fair way.**

◎ **If you believe that you are a victim in an unfair, discriminatory, or challenging situation and decide to do nothing to help yourself, it can have a long-lasting negative impact on your whole life.**

◎ **If you do not decide on self-advocacy, you will miss out on the incredible learning experience that takes place when you stick up for yourself in a legal and orderly way.**

◎ **Teens participated in the antiwar movement and became involved in civil rights issues.**

◎ **Teens fought along with adults for nationwide social change and for changes in the local schools.**

◎ **Teens advocated for control of their bodies, access to birth control, and expanded legal rights.**

◎ **Teens were involved in getting the voting age reduced to eighteen.**

Teen efforts in the 1960s changed laws and attitudes. Their efforts also expanded and changed the services available to teens because they became a force that needed attention. Teens in the 1960s showed that schools, colleges, and the courts needed to see them as individual citizens with rights as well as responsibilities. They showed that teens had value as intelligent young people, not just as potential adults.

As a result of the protests of the 1960s, there are youth services available to a wide range of teens who have specific needs: those in foster care; runaways; those with health problems; those who are pregnant or who need birth control counseling; students with learning disabilities; and those who believe they are discriminated against because of their race, religion, or sexual orientation, to name a few. Services were not always available for teens in these situations. The youth services organizations that existed in the 1960s expected conformity and obedience. The 1960s were a potent time for change, and adults were forced to take notice.

Gerald Gault was a fifteen-year-old Arizona teenager on June 8, 1964, when he was arrested for allegedly making an obscene phone call to a neighbor. Gerald was taken from his home without his parents' knowledge. When his parents returned home, they had no idea where Gerald was. They finally found him at the children's detention center. Gerald's parents argued that their son had been denied his due process rights, but the judge in the original case did not agree. The judge said that Gerald needed the protection of the court because he was under age eighteen and a delinquent minor. Gerald was found guilty and committed to a state industrial school until age twenty-one—a sentence of six years. An adult charged with a similar crime would have paid a fine of fifty dollars and two months in jail.

In 1965, John Tinker was fifteen years old and upset about the Vietnam War. He and other teenagers planned to protest the war by fasting and wearing black armbands to school. The school heard of the plan and told the students they had to remove their armbands or be sent home until they did. John Tinker, his sister Mary Beth, and Chris Eckhardt wore the armbands despite the order and were suspended.

John Tinker.

In 2006, John Tinker continues to be involved in protests and in youth advocacy efforts. He says, "We didn't recognize what [this case] would become when we did it. We were protesting the Vietnam War, not free speech, but it became a free speech case. We were motivated by a strong sense of the immorality of the war. I talk to students occasionally and try to motivate them to pay attention. I want students to know that what happens today and what they do today brings about what the future will be like and shapes our world tomorrow."

Decisions made by the U.S. Supreme Court were involved in the country's attitude change. The court handed down two important rulings in the 1960s that changed the way teens could be treated. In *In Re Gault* (1967) the court ruled that the Fourteenth Amendment to the Constitution applies to juveniles. The court said that juveniles have the right to know the charges against them, that they have the right to be represented by a lawyer, and the right to confront witnesses. They also must be told of their right not to testify against themselves.

In *Tinker v. Des Moines Independent School District* (1968), the Supreme Court ruled that the First Amendment guarantees of free speech apply to students. It was ruled that the students in the case could not be prohibited from wearing black armbands to protest the Vietnam War. The majority opinion stated that students, whether they are in school or out, are "persons" under the Constitution.

Decisions in the 1960s were followed by other Supreme Court decisions that furthered the rights of teens. In the case of *Goss v. Lopez* (1975), the Supreme Court ruled that students had the right to a hearing before a school suspension. This ruling, which changed the history of school government, reinforced the idea that teens were protected by the Fourteenth Amendment and could not be denied liberty without due process. In *Board of Education v. Pico* (1982), the court ruled again on the rights of free speech. The court's decision held that books could not be removed from a school library because students needed access to ideas to help them become responsible citizens.

Not all Supreme Court cases came down on the side of teens' rights, but issues related to young people were (and are still) heard in the Supreme Court on the same level as adult issues. Youths are seen as people deserving of rights and respect. Their voices are heard, and their concerns are given serious consideration. Teens in the 1960s worked hard to gain rights and respect. They left an important legacy but not an entitlement. Attitudes about teenagers change constantly. The rights teens enjoy right now also can change.

Teens of every generation must continue to advocate, to negotiate, and to define the issues that affect them personally and affect the world they live in. When you advocate for yourself, you call on many resources, resources within yourself,

"Being your own advocate is not easy. What is? However, it is important for a number of reasons. The first reason, and by far the most important reason, is that nobody knows what you truly need to be successful better than you do. Who can understand better than you can what your academic life is like? What is a little difficult for you to do, and what is impossible? You know what works for you and you know what doesn't. Cutting out the middleman can mean cutting out miscommunication, confusion, and frustration."—Melissa, age seventeen and resources that are available to you in organizations in your community, state, and even in the federal government. Those resources will be detailed in the rest of this book.

If you need to know about laws that can help you, many government and other organizations can help you identify laws that have been enacted against prejudice and against barriers that prevent full and equal participation. The laws are there to protect you from discrimination and to ensure your rights as a citizen.

BE FULLY INFORMED BEFORE YOU BEGIN YOUR ADVOCACY

Melissa.

In the 1960s, the Supreme Court ruled that young people, not just adults, have constitutional rights. The laws that protect your rights are the basis for the advocacy issues included in this book. If the issue you need to address is not directly connected to the law, there are other resources that might be just as useful to help you in your situation. It is important to know what resources are out there and how to access them, and this book will provide you with that information. If you are still not sure whether you can or should begin self-advocacy, take the short quiz at the end of this chapter. If you answer *yes* to most of the questions, you will want to explore the options available to you and then to begin your self-advocacy effort.

Advocacy will not change who you are. It will not make your disability, if you have one, disappear. Advocacy will not necessarily get you out of trouble with the law or your school if you have done something illegal or against school rules. Advocacy will not make the impossible possible, and it will not always make you popular—sometimes, in fact, it may make you unpopular, at least for a while. Advocacy will, however, change the way you see your world and your place in it.

When you advocate for yourself, you will develop a plan and follow through on that plan toward a positive conclusion. If you have never spoken up for yourself before, this book will help you learn how to do it in a dignified, organized, and legal way. When you advocate for yourself, you not only are taking steps to right the wrong you have been facing but also adding to your knowledge of how to take care of yourself. The sooner you learn to speak up for yourself as a teen, the sooner you will be able to live independently. When you learn to do this as a teen, you will be better able to speak up for yourself, when needed, as an adult.

SHOULD I BEGIN SELF-ADVOCACY?

If most of my answers are *yes*, then it's time to begin!

1. Do I have a realistic project or a dream that remains unaccomplished?
2. Do I sometimes feel overwhelmed or intimidated because of prejudices or barriers in my school or in my community?
3. Do I believe I am being denied access to educational, recreational, or employment opportunities?
4. Do I know of accommodations that would make it easier to go to school or do my job but are not available to me?
5. Are there barriers to my full participation in my life with my friends after school?
6. Do I fear that I will be denied admission to the college or job opportunity of my choice because of prejudice or barriers?
7. Do I believe that my home situation, either with my biological parents or foster parents, is unsafe?
8. Do I worry about the risky activities my friends try to get me involved in and whether I will get arrested, pregnant, infected with a sexually transmitted disease (STD), or physically hurt?

How to Self-Advocate

"THE FIRST STEP IS ALWAYS THE HARDEST. . . ."

If we were to tell you self-advocacy would be easy, we would be misleading you. Advocating for yourself takes courage. It takes courage just to realize that you must act to get what you need, are entitled to, and deserve. If you have taken the quiz in chapter 1 and answered *yes* to most of the questions, then you know the time has come to act on your own behalf—to start self-advocacy. It's natural to feel nervous, even when you know that self-advocacy is the right thing to do.

Getting organized will help. This chapter gives you several step-by-step tools to use in planning your self-advocacy project. We provide you with an approach to use when you are negotiating with the appropriate decision-making authority to achieve your goals. We help you learn how to decide when and if to involve the media in your self-advocacy project. Then, chapter 3 gives you detailed information on effectively dealing with the media. Along the way, we give you resources to use and tips to follow that will help make your project successful.

Keep in mind that even if this chapter doesn't specifically address the issue or issues you face, you can adapt the tools in the chapter to your situation. You can use the chapter as a starting point, then read the issue-specific chapters for detailed information. So, first, take a deep breath, and ask yourself, "Where do I begin?"

TAKING THAT FIRST STEP

The most important first step is deciding that, yes, you will be your own advocate. You will not be a victim, you will speak up, you will start a dialogue about the issues you face, and you will work toward resolving your situation. Once you make your decision to be a self-advocate, try to start by talking with a trusted friend or adult about your feelings and the results you want to achieve.

There are probably many things that concern you about your situation. If you attempt to deal with all your concerns at once, it will be easy to become confused, anxious, and overwhelmed. However, if you start by finding a focus and then take the following steps, your self-advocacy project will feel much more doable. Here is a quick overview of each step to take. Each step is fully explained throughout the chapter.

- ◎ **Focus first.** Choose the one aspect of your situation that is the most important to you and concentrate on that issue. You may discover that the other issues concerning you will be dealt with as you resolve the most important one.

- ◎ **Choose a goal.** Think about what you really want to happen as a result of your self-advocacy and make that your goal. When

Writing things down, by hand or on a computer, can make the following steps seem much easier and clearer and will help you set priorities. For example, when you are focusing on which issue is most important to you, try listing all the things you believe are a barrier to you, then give each one a number value to narrow down your choices. If you have a disability that makes it hard to write, find a trusted person to be your "scribe."

setting your goals, consider both results that can be achieved in the short term and long-term goals that may take a year or more to achieve.

- Depersonalize. This might be the most important step of all! Before you write or say one word, be sure that everything you say will help you reach your goal. Taking it personally, that is, thinking that the problem is a direct attack on you, will make it more difficult to find a resolution. Stick with the facts that support your goal.

- Research. Gather information and learn your rights. Make sure you know what laws, contracts, or regulations apply in your situation. If no laws are being violated, but you believe your situation is unfair, immoral, or wrong, concentrate on what would be an acceptable, realistic solution to your issue.

- Know your audience. Find out who or what group can give you what you need. For example, if your problem is at school, could it be resolved by talking to a teacher or the school principal? Or will you have to talk with the school district superintendent or the school board?

- Know your audience's needs. How will your request affect the people you need to address? Can you persuade the person or group that by helping you, a broader situation can be improved?

Self-advocacy takes more time than speaking or acting impulsively. When you are in an upsetting situation, taking these steps may seem overwhelming or even a waste of time, but taking these steps doesn't always mean spending days to plan ahead. If you have a trusted friend or advisor to help you, it may take only a few minutes or a few hours to put a plan in place. You will discover that when you organize your thoughts and actions, you will have a much better chance of resolving your issues.

The Young Women's Project (YWP) in Washington, D.C., was founded in 1992 to help build female teen leaders. YWP's programs include self-advocacy and leadership training, employment opportunities, and project work to enable teens to educate and organize their peers to work to change laws and policies. YWP's Teen Women in Action (TWA) is an after-school leadership program. Teen women involved with YWP have made a difference in their schools, their community, and their own lives:

- "I like being involved with the community and changing things, like my environment and my peers. I like having a voice."—Kathy, Wilson High School senior, Washington, D.C.
- "Working with TWA taught me useful skills, like how to interview and collect and analyze data. I can take those into my professional life and make a big impact."—Jasmin, Wilson High School junior, Washington, D.C.

- Know what to say. If you want to change something that is unfair, illegal, immoral, or wrong, be sure that what you say and how you say it are persuasive and nonthreatening. Decide on a "message" and stay with it. We explain what messages are in this chapter and in chapter 3.
- Know how and where to deliver your message. In public or in private? One-on-one or in a meeting? Should you hold a press conference, organize a demonstration, or start picketing?
- Use the right messenger. Are you the right person to ask for what you need or should you choose a spokesperson? If you are working with a group, always choose one person to be the messenger.
- Know when and how to use the media. The media can be a powerful tool in drawing attention to your issue, especially if you

believe the decision makers have not heard your message or are ignoring your goals. It is important, however, to know when and how to involve the media (see chapter 3).

Focus First

Sure, it seems difficult to sort through all the things that feel wrong about your situation and then choose the most important thing. It's important to trust your instincts about how you feel. So, first, make a list.

Your list should include all the ways that your situation feels wrong to you. Make sure to name every specific physical, procedural, or perceived barrier or behavior you encounter in your situation. If you believe you are being discriminated against or harassed, it is important to be specific about who is doing the discrimination and what actions or words have made you feel harassed. For example: Your disability requires you to use a wheelchair or a device to help you walk. There are areas of your school that are difficult, if not impossible, for you to gain access to. List all of those areas. Then choose which of those areas is the most critical to your success at school. Are you interested in science, but the science labs are on the second floor with no elevator in the building? What about the school's bathrooms—are they accessible to you? Are the hallways too narrow for you to move through them in a timely way between classes? List all of these barriers, and then select the one that affects you the most (the one that, more than any other one, prevents you from reaching your scholastic goals).

Try hard not to become frustrated by this step—it is the first exercise in a process that will lead to your getting what you need to succeed.

Choose a Goal

If the world were a perfect place, all people would be treated fairly and be given the education and jobs they deserve, no matter what their abilities, race, religious beliefs, gender, or national origin. If the world were a perfect place, the need for self-advocacy would be rare, and you wouldn't need this book!

Sadly, the world is far from perfect, and you wouldn't be reading this book if you weren't in a situation that you think is unfair, illegal, immoral, or wrong. You want the world, or at least your corner of it, to change—but how? What do you think should happen to your situation so that the major issue you're focusing on will improve and be resolved? The process we describe is called *goal setting*.

Once again, start by making a list, writing down the ways that your everyday life could be improved if your situation could change. Start out by brainstorming—thinking of all the ideas you can without making a judgment about any of them. Once you have your list, cross off the solutions that are completely unrealistic. Then make a check mark next to the resolutions that you think might be possible to achieve. You might be able to accomplish some of those resolutions quickly if your self-advocacy project is successful. These may be called your short-term goals.

Other resolutions might be realistic to achieve but also might take more time to accomplish. Call these your long-term goals. If you have trouble or are being abused at home, it may be crucial that you find a temporary place to live to protect yourself or your siblings from further harm. Advocating for a temporary home would be your short-term goal. Eventually, however, you may want your family reunited and living together safely. Reaching that resolution could take intensive counseling, including possible substance abuse treatment, anger management education, or even legal intervention. Because the process of reuniting your family is necessarily slow, it would be a long-term goal.

Try brainstorming with a sympathetic friend or trusted adult to expand the possible ideas. If your self-advocacy project is a group effort, you're certain to get plenty of ideas.

After you have reviewed possible outcomes, choose the one short-term and one long-term goal that you will concentrate on in your self-advocacy project. From now on, you will focus on the most important issue in your situation.

Depersonalize

If the problem you want to advocate against is personal, why do you need to depersonalize? If you see your situation as a direct, personal attack on you, your audience will see you as a victim and not as a self-advocate. The more you see your issues from a victim's point of view, the angrier and more frustrated you will become, and the less effective your statements and requests will be.

To depersonalize, try viewing your situation as if it were happening to another person. Try to look at your situation as if you were observing what is happening. Then, look at your situation as if you are the one who can bring about a resolution. Often, if the situation is especially frustrating and upsetting, depersonalizing an issue may require that you get help from a capable friend, a sympathetic adult, or a counselor. To give yourself a different perspective on your situation, walk the issue through, or do role-plays in which you switch identities. Do this until you can convert the energy of your anger into the energy of successful self-advocacy.

Shelby Knox, a teen in Lubbock, Texas, made it her goal to educate her conservative community about the "facts of life," that is, reality-based sexuality education. Shelby's efforts led to the filming of an award-winning movie, *The Education of Shelby Knox*. Read about Shelby's advocacy efforts in chapter 8.

- Successful self-advocates see that if an unfair situation can happen to them, it can happen to anyone.
- Successful self-advocates speak up for themselves while focusing on the issues, not on themselves as victims.
- Successful self-advocates have a strong, clear message.
- Successful self-advocates may speak forcefully at times and are not afraid to show how they feel about their situation, but they never speak in anger publicly.

◎ **Successful self-advocates never lose sight of their goal, which is to find a resolution to their situation.**

The more you make your self-advocacy about the unfairness of a situation, the more successful you will be. The more you focus your self-advocacy globally rather than personally, the easier it will be for your audience to relate to your goals.

Research—Gather Information and Learn Your Rights

As you read in chapter 1, teen and adult advocates have been successful in persuading legislators to write laws that protect the rights of youth, women, the disabled, and many other groups. Title IX, to name one influential law, has had a major impact on the athletic and other school programs that are now available to women and girls. In addition, the Supreme Court has decided that certain rights are protected by the U.S. Constitution, even when those rights are not specifically mentioned. For example, they have ruled that the right to privacy is protected by the Constitution, and, in many cases, that the right to privacy should extend to young people, even in schools.

In addition to Supreme Court decisions and federal laws, state and local laws and regulations may apply to your situation. Your school or place of employment may be operating under a contract that is being violated by the treatment you are receiving. If you believe your rights or those of your group are being violated, many organizations are available to help, either by providing information or by offering direct assistance. The American Civil Liberties Union (ACLU), for example, is dedicated to protecting the civil rights of every citizen and offers specific help for young people. See the ACLU website at www.aclu.org/studentsrights/index.html.

Stick to fact-based sites sponsored by the government, hospitals, and official organizations to find out what laws apply, and read the actual text of the laws themselves. If there are discussion sites or unofficial advocacy sites related to your

The Internet makes researching laws and regulations easy and provides a great way to get ideas. Even if you don't have a computer at home, your school or public library will have computers with Internet access that you can use for your research. You can start a search for information at one of the easiest sites to use, such as Google, Ask.com, About.com, Factopia, or Wikipedia. Type in either a word or phrase related to your issue, such as "disabled access" or the name of the law, such as "Title IX," and the search engine will find a variety of related sites to visit.

issue, read through some of them to get an idea of what others in your situation have been able to accomplish. Always be aware, however, that statements on advocacy sites and in blogs may be inaccurate.

You should be able to access back issues of your local newspapers if you need to research public agreements, policies, or contracts that affect your school system or community. The newspaper office might have actual copies of back issues to read through, or they may be available online. If back issues are destroyed or timed out online, most libraries keep a file of back issues to review on microfilm or microfiche. You will need to ask the librarian to help you access such files. Public boards and commissions are required to keep the minutes of their meetings for the public to review, and those minutes might be useful in finding information that will help in resolving your situation. The resource lists at the end of each chapter will provide you with a number of helpful websites for gathering information. All of the sites listed will provide accurate facts and statistics.

Teens for Safe Cosmetics, a group that got started to do a high
school project on cancer rates in their California community,
did its research and was able to persuade the state
government to pass a law requiring cosmetics companies to
list all potentially cancer-causing ingredients on product labels.
Read about Teens for Safe Cosmetics in chapter 4.

If no laws are being violated, but you believe your situation
is unfair, immoral, or wrong, concentrate on what would be a
fair, realistic solution to your issue. In addition to the ACLU,
there may be organizations or professional individuals (such as
attorneys who specialize in assisting young people) in your
area. Such groups or professional adults can help you find
assistance in focusing your issue, choosing a goal, and
presenting your situation and proposed resolution to the
decision-making authority. In the issue-related chapters of this
book, we provide you with information about specific groups
to contact when you need assistance in resolving those issues.

Know Your Audience

At this point in preparing your self-advocacy project, it's
probably clear who you need to persuade to accomplish your
goal. To be sure you're on the right track, however, figure out
the chain of command of the decision-making power in your
situation. That may be simple. For example, you may feel that
your work shift is either too long or too short or at an
inconvenient time of day, and you want to have your hours
changed. Your audience may be just one person, perhaps the
shift supervisor at the store where you work. If that's the case, it
will be important to find out what hours that person works,
where his or her office is located (if there is an office), and, if
possible, when that person might be available to meet with you.
Once you know these things, leave that person a note or make a
telephone call to make sure he or she is available when you can
come in to make your presentation.

If you work closely with the supervisor, you might know things about him or her that will help you present your case. Is he or she patient or impatient? Will your presentation to him or her have to be fast and to the point? Is he or she a young person going to school while he or she works or a parent with lots of responsibilities at home? The more you know, the more you can tailor your approach to his or her needs. It may be better for the supervisor if you are informal when you make your request, or if the supervisor needs approval for decisions, it may be best if you write down in detail what you need and why you need it.

It's important to consider your next step, as well. If the shift supervisor turns down your request for a change in hours, will that end your self-advocacy project or is there someone you can speak to who is a step or two above in the chain of command? If you go to someone higher in the chain of command, be sure the shift supervisor knows that you intend to do so. Some supervisors resent someone "going over their head." If the situation is important to you—if you really want to keep the job or have hopes of advancement in the company—it could be worth the risk to speak to a person in a higher management position.

There may come a time, if your self-advocacy situation involves your school system, for example, that you will need to skip ahead through the chain of command. If the first person you speak with refers you to a higher decision-making authority, it is important to know your audience each step of the way. First you might start talking to a teacher or the school principal, then to the local school committee, and on up to a large, powerful group, such as your state's commission on education. In each case, try to find out as much as you can about each person or group. If it is a committee you must meet with, find out when the group meets, who serves on the committee, whether the members of the committee have children in your school, or whether some of them donate large amounts of money to your school. In each and every case along the way, you will need to know how to make an appointment; how to get yourself placed on the agenda (list of topics in the order in which they will be addressed) of a meeting; when the best time is to approach the person or group; whether to make a formal or informal presentation; and what backup materials to bring along to help present your case.

Know Your Audience's Needs

When you are focused on your own needs and goals, it's difficult to imagine that the person or group that has the most influence on your self-advocacy project has needs and goals as well. Most people live complicated lives, whether at home or at work—even powerful people. Committees, boards, and commissions have many details to consider with every decision they make. Organizations have strict budgets and must accomplish many things without overspending those budgets.

Your issue deserves to be treated with respect by each person or group you talk with to achieve your goal. By the same token, you must treat each person or group you meet with respect and take the person or group's needs into account. For example, imagine that the barrier you face in your school can be eliminated, but it will require a multimillion-dollar renovation or rebuilding project to do so. It's important to know that whenever any type of construction occurs on a public building, all aspects of that building must be brought into compliance with Americans with Disabilities Act (ADA) codes.

Imagine that in your community getting approval for school-building renovations has been extremely difficult—the taxpayers have voted down several efforts to build a new school. How do you think the school committee in your town would react to your proposal to meet your goals, if the board members think your plan might result in cutting back on your school's programs to make the school meet ADA requirements? Is it possible for you to present a plan that would meet the school committee's goals as well? That scenario could present a situation where having both short-term goals and long-term goals isuseful. There may be a less expensive, temporary solution that will remove some of the barriers you face. Achieving your short-term goal will give you time to work hard on achieving your long-term goal. For example, in your research, you might be able to find grant money that is available to schools that renovate to remove barriers to the physically handicapped. The money might make it possible to make lasting changes that will not only remove your barriers but make achieving a barrier-free education possible for generations of young people in the years ahead.

Sometimes, knowing your audience can involve something as simple as being aware of your shift supervisor's school schedule. If, in your request to change your hours, you can suggest that you start work at a time when he or she needs to leave for a night class, the supervisor might be more likely to grant your request. Each situation you face in your self-advocacy projects will require that you pay attention to the needs of the person or group who can make your goals a reality. When you make it clear in all your discussions that you have considered not only your needs but also theirs, you will find that your audience is much more receptive to your requests. The more successful you are at getting to know your audience, the more successful your self-advocacy will be.

Know What to Say

Everyone needs a message—not only to know what to say but also to have a clue about how to say it. If you want that shift change, for example, you'd better decide how to approach your shift supervisor. Will you say, "Yo, I got games every weekend, so I can't work Saturday nights"? Or will you have done your homework and know your audience, so you're aware that the shift supervisor loves sports and is working his or her way through college? If you've done that research, you might also know that the store has been advertising for help on Sunday afternoons. So a more effective message will be to tell the shift supervisor that you value your job and like your work. You think you can get a basketball scholarship to college, so you need to practice and play in school games on weekends. Because that conflicts with your current work schedule, can you work Sunday afternoons instead of Saturday nights?

If you're making a presentation before a governing body or holding a press conference, it's even more critical that your message and the way you express yourself are focused and well thought out. Many ears and eyes will be paying attention to you, and it's easy for people to misunderstand your purpose and goals if you aren't clear. In a formal presentation, decide what visual aids, like graphics, charts, statistics, and photographs, will help illustrate your point and make your goal even more apparent to your audience. Most important, just as you did when you were at the first step and coming up with a focus, decide on the few major points you want to get across.

Simply put, you will want to:

- State your issue—use graphics and photos to help if you like.
- Give an example of what isn't working in your situation, again illustrating with photos if you have them.
- Say what you think should happen—state your goals, and briefly explain how you came up with your solution. Here is where offering short-term and long-term solutions will help show that you want to improve the situation not just for yourself but for everyone.

When you have finished your presentation, be prepared for questions. Again, knowing your audience will help you get ready for questioning. If you know that members of the governing board can be aggressive, be sure that you have depersonalized, so you can answer factually, without anger or extreme emotion. It's not necessary to make your presentation and answers flat and completely lacking in emotion. Avoid raising your voice, avoid sarcasm, and try to avoid tears!

Know How and Where to Deliver Your Message

Doing your research will help you figure out the best time and place to present your goal. Again, many factors will be involved, depending on whether you will be making a one-on-one presentation or a more formal presentation to a governing body. For example, if you are depending on your shift supervisor to change your work hours, it will be important to find a time that is convenient for him or her to talk about your schedule. If you get to know his or her routine and know when his or her day is busiest, you can call ahead to ask if you can meet for a few minutes at, say, 11:30 A.M. Ask if you can meet in a conference room or a break room that will be empty at that time. Be on time, be ready with the reasons for your request, and be polite. If the first answer is *no*, have compromise solutions ready to present. Then no matter what the answer is, thank the supervisor for his or her time. If you plan to present your request to a supervisor or another person with more authority, state your intention politely and respectfully, not in anger and definitely not in an "I'll-show-you!" attitude. Instead, make it clear that the job is important to you, and you hope things can work out to benefit both you and your supervisor.

Committees and other decision-making authorities usually meet at specific times at regularly scheduled meetings. In most cases, committees follow an agenda, and topics on the agenda will be allotted a specific length of time for presentations and discussion. Most committees will have a secretary or administrative assistant who prepares the agenda and makes copies of background materials for committee members. Find out who the administrator for your committee is, and contact him or her to be given a slot on the agenda to present your issue and goals. In some cases, the administrator may be able to provide equipment to show your charts, graphics, or photos, but be prepared to have your own equipment ready to display whatever materials you need to support your goal. In addition, be sure to have plenty of copies made to distribute to the committee, the audience, and the media (see chapter 3).

It might be necessary to contact a committee member to get permission for a time slot on the committee's agenda. If that's the case, if you are not the group spokesperson, it may be wise to ask your spokesperson to make the contact. That way, if the committee member starts an informal discussion of your situation before the meeting, the spokesperson can be ready to explain the major points you will make at the meeting.

Choose the Right Messenger

Not all people speak well in public or when they are under stress. If your issue is a personal one that you must resolve yourself, it will be important to practice what you want to say and the way you need to say it. In all cases, you will want to be polite, direct, and stay with your message. If you have a disability that means your speech is not easily understood, it will be wise to find a trusted friend or adult who understands your situation to speak on your behalf. Have at least one meeting with the person who will speak for you to be sure that everything he or she will say reflects what is important to you about your issue and your goals. You will have to decide if you want your spokesperson to negotiate for you; when you meet, be sure you are clear about how much you want to empower your spokesperson to say without first having to confer with you.

If your situation involves a group, it is important that one person be chosen as spokesperson for the group. The spokesperson does not have to be the person who is also the leader of your group. However, the spokesperson should be someone who is trustworthy, is dedicated to your group's issues and goals, and who has become educated enough about the group's message to answer questions in a way that reflects the group's intentions. Be sure that the spokesperson you choose is readily available and easy to contact. It is a huge mistake to choose a spokesperson who travels a lot or keeps his or her cell phone turned off most of the time!

Know When and How to Use the Media

If you find that your attempts to start a dialogue about your issue are falling flat, that your request to be placed on the agenda of a board meeting is denied, or that your point of view about your issue is not being respected, it may be time to involve the media. Before deciding to involve the media in your issue, read chapter 3 thoroughly. Be sure you know what can happen when the media throws its bright lights on your issue.

Of course, you won't make a call or send a press release to the media if your shift supervisor won't let you change your

Jennifer Boccia of Allen, Texas, used the media in her self-advocacy project. Jennifer and fifteen of her friends were told by school administrators that they must stop wearing black armbands to protest strict school policies set up after the Columbine High School shootings in Littleton, Colorado. With the help of media attention and legal assistance from the ACLU, Jennifer and her friends took their issue to court. The media and legal pressure led the school district to settle the matter in Jennifer's favor. Read about Jennifer in chapter 5.

work hours. But if you are fired from a job because your employer refuses to make a reasonable accommodation to your disability, that could present an opportunity to use the media to make others aware of something that is unfair, illegal, immoral, or wrong. In the process, media attention may help resolve your issue if the public sees the story and puts pressure on your employer to change its policies. Making your issue known to the public can help others in your situation avoid future discrimination.

If your local school board refuses to hear your presentation or dismisses your issue as unimportant, the media can help. When the public sees the lack of respect you have received,

Always remember your goals: You want to resolve your situation, not make it worse! Think through the potential impact of media involvement on the decision-making authority you want to persuade. Know your audience! Will bringing the media into the situation make the person or group more or less likely to listen to what you have to say?

27

There are many resources available to help you learn negotiating skills. One of the most famous, because it is so successful, is the book *Getting to YES: Negotiating Agreement without Giving In*. The book was first written in the 1980s but is still in print because the concepts work, and people use them every day. You might also look at *The Handbook of Dispute Resolution*, a more recent book that was written by members of the Harvard Negotiating Project (www.pon.harvard.edu/hnp).

NEGOTIATING

Not all conversations go easily. When you prepare a message about your situation and goals, remember that the person or group you're speaking to might object. If the person or group is a decision-making authority, the first answer to your request may be *no*. But, even if the first answer you get is *no*, you don't want to give up on resolving your issue. *No* is an answer that is often unfair and arbitrary. Taking *no* for an answer will end your self-advocacy and could prompt frustration, resentment, and feelings of victimhood.

Negotiation is an important self-advocacy tool. If you learn and practice negotiating skills, you will be a more effective self-advocate. A useful strategy to combat a negative response is to include answers to possible objections in your preparation. Your goal in any negotiation is a wise agreement, one that benefits all parties while accomplishing your goal. The book *Getting to YES* defines a wise agreement as one that: "meets the legitimate interests of each side to the extent possible, resolves conflicting interests fairly, is durable, and takes community interests into account" (p. 4).

The steps used in negotiating based on *Getting to YES* are:

- Don't bargain over positions: Negotiate the merits of the issue. In "principled negotiation," both sides become problem-solvers.
- Separate the people from the problem: Depersonalize! When you do this, you focus on the issue that must be resolved.
- Focus on interests, not positions: Never go into a negotiation with demands and a "bottom line." Remain flexible; that doesn't mean being soft, it means being open to creative solutions to your issue.
- Invent options for mutual gain: Work with the other side to come up with several options that might resolve the issue. Which one you both choose can be decided as discussions continue.
- Insist on using objective criteria: Set standards in your negotiation. Make sure it does not become a contest of one strong will against another. Reason should prevail, not pressure from either side.

In this book, we can't explore all of the reasons why negotiation works best when approached in a principled way. For case studies and more details about principled negotiation, go online or check *Getting to YES* out of the library.

people may put public pressure on the board. Successful media involvement may result in your issue and goals receiving the attention they deserve.

If you hold a demonstration, such as picketing your school or marching to the school board's office, be sure everyone involved in the demonstration is "on the same page" with your goals and pledges to be polite and well behaved. Then and only then, invite the media to attend. Make sure your spokesperson will be at your event, and make sure everyone else who attends knows to refer questions from the media to your spokesperson. Once you invite the media to attend and cover your issue, everything that happens can be reported. You want good attention about your issue, not negative attention. Remember your goals, and stick to your message!

Chapters 4 through 10 provide you with detailed and specific information about issues you may face in your life. Each chapter offers examples of teens like you who used self-advocacy tools to resolve difficult situations. The issue-oriented chapters give you more of a foundation to advocate for yourself. However, the book is designed so that if you have an urgent need to read about a problem affecting you right now, you can read the first three chapters and then apply the information in a specific issue-oriented chapter to your situation.

Good luck on your path to self-advocacy!

RESOURCES

◎ **The Young Women's Project, Washington, D.C.:**
www.youngwomensproject.org

◎ **The Meyer Foundation: www.meyerfoundation.org**

◎ **Harvard Negotiating Project, Roger Fisher, Director:**
www.pon.harvard.edu/hnp

3 Dealing with the Media

If you believe that resolving your issue requires you to contact the media, there are some basic rules to follow to be sure you are using the power of the press effectively and in your best interest. First and foremost, keep these concepts in mind once you decide to contact the media in trying to resolve your situation (see chapter 2):

- **The media is not your enemy.**
- **The media is not your friend.**
- **Always be cautious and "on message" when you speak with the media.**

Reporters who talk to you about your issue will be talking to you because that is their job. This will be true whether they are writers from a local weekly newspaper or from a large metropolitan daily paper, whether they are from a network affiliate television station or radio news station, or the local cable news show or student radio news show. They have been assigned to cover your situation by their editors, who are their bosses. Whether or not they seem sympathetic to your point of view does not, and should not, matter—the best reporters will tell both sides of every story fairly, whether they agree with one side and oppose the other or not.

If your issue is an emotional one, be even more aware of what you say to the media, and prepare yourself or your spokesperson even more carefully. Media consultants have made millions of dollars helping large corporations—and important politicians—"fix" mistakes they made when they let emotion take over their public words, and they forgot their message. Tears and anger make great sound bites; but it is unlikely that losing your temper while you are talking with the media will do anything to help resolve your issue in a positive way (see chapter 2).

Now you know that you need to stay cautious at all times. Here are the basics of using the media:

- **Know who and what your media outlets are; that is, find out which newspapers, radio stations, and television stations cover your area.**
- **Know which media outlets will be the most likely to cover your issue (for example, a large network television station is less likely to cover a local story in a small community).**
- **Decide the best way to contact the media (that is, by phone, with a press release, by a letter to the editor, or an op-ed article).**
- **Decide who will be your spokesperson (this is especially important if you have a disability that affects your speech or if you are part of a group).**
- **Decide which part of your issue is the most important to convey to the media.**
- **Come up with three or at most four phrases or sentences that explain your issue and express the reasons why it is important that your issue be resolved.**

WRITE A LETTER OR OPINION ARTICLE

There are many times when a well-written letter to the editor or op-ed article will be the best way to alert a large audience about your issue. Say that you decide not to make a public presentation to your local school board. Instead, you want to persuade the members of the community to support your goals, so that they will pressure the board to make a decision that will resolve your situation. A well-written letter to the editor or op-ed article can be effective in such a situation.

First, check with the editor of your local newspaper for the paper's guidelines and rules about letters. In most cases, letters to the editor are required to be between two and three hundred words and must not libel anyone (simply, libel is written and slander is spoken, and both are false statements that cause harm to a person). It's important that you avoid angry words and especially important that you avoid any personal attacks in your letter. Make your letter organized and concise, clearly state your issue, and say what you think should happen to resolve your situation. A letter is most likely to be printed if it is fair, clear, and within the word number limits that the paper sets for submissions. An op-ed (opposite the editorial page) article can be slightly longer, but usually you will need to get approval from the newspaper's editor to write it and have it published.

WRITE A PRESS RELEASE

If you or your group decides that you want to make a public appearance, you will want to write a press release to alert the media that there is an event they will want to cover. If you are going to make a presentation to the school board, for example, make sure that you are placed on the board's agenda for the night you want to speak. You do not want to invite media to the meeting if you will not be allowed to make your presentation. If, rather than making a formal presentation, you want to organize a press conference, a demonstration, or a picket line, be sure you know what type of activity is allowed on public and private property in your community. It is important that you have tried every other avenue before you explore civil disobedience—getting arrested makes great headlines, but again, it is unlikely to get you the resolution you seek.

How to Write a Press Release

Writing a press release can be easy if you follow some basic rules:

- ◎ **Keep it simple.**
- ◎ **Keep it short.**
- ◎ **Keep it to the point.**
- ◎ **Always include who, what, when, where, and why (the five Ws)**

As a student journalist working for your school newspaper or television station, you are a member of the media. Just like a professional journalist, you must present the news accurately, fairly, and impartially. Your editorials must be accurate and avoid libeling any person or group. You must follow guidelines set by your editors, such as your school's newspaper advisor or the school principal.

As a student journalist, you may decide to self-advocate when they think your school's administration isn't "advising" so much as "censoring" your work. Organizations, such as the American Civil Liberties Union (ACLU) and the Student Press Law Center (SPLC), can help. SPLC is a legal assistance agency devoted to educating high school and college journalists "about the rights and responsibilities embodied in the First Amendment and supporting the student news media in their struggle to cover important issues free from censorship" (from www.splc.org/about.asp). SPLC was founded by John Tinker, the student whose self-advocacy led to the Supreme Court decision *Tinker v. Des Moines Independent School District* (see chapter 5).

Katy Dean successfully challenged her school's censorship of an article she wrote for her Utica, Michigan, high school paper in March 2002. For her efforts, Katy received the SPLC's Courage in Journalism award in 2003 and said "My case has helped me realize that the First Amendment is not some far-off ideal that was fought for hundreds of years ago, but a significant right that we need to fight for every day."

You'll want to send a press release to the media to alert them to something you have done or are going to do about your situation. Either you will want the press release to be printed so that the public will come to your event, or you will want the press to cover your event, or in many cases, you will want both these things to happen. So, if you keep the press release simple and stick to the facts, you are more likely to achieve your goals. In the text of the press release:

- Clearly state your issue in one sentence.
- Give an example of why the issue is important and how it is affecting you and/or your group.
- Say what you think should be the solution.

- State when and where you will be making your presentation to the decision-making authority involved.
- State when and where you will be making a public statement, holding a rally, or picketing about your issue.
- Provide your spokesperson's phone number for reporters to call and make sure that person is prepared (using the steps previously discussed) to talk.

It's important that your spokesperson is available to answer calls. There are few more frustrating things to a reporter than getting a story assignment and not being able to reach the primary contact.

KNOW YOUR MEDIA AND DEADLINES

When you send out your press release, be sure you are sending it at the time and in the format that the media outlet wants to receive it. For example, many newspapers want press releases sent to a dedicated e-mail address for a specific department. Many television and radio stations like to receive their press releases by fax, to a number that is monitored by a news editor or assignment editor.

It's important to know the deadlines (the last day that submissions are accepted before printing or broadcast) of the media outlets you are contacting. If you live in a smaller community where the main news comes from a weekly newspaper, make sure you time your letter or press release to arrive well before the next issue is printed. If you don't, you'll have to wait another whole week before your news can get out to your audience. If the newspaper prints on Wednesday, make sure the editors have your letter or press release no later than Monday morning. For daily newspapers, find out the name of the editor who will read your letter or press release and send it directly to that person.

Follow the same basic guidelines for radio and television stations. In many places, the local cable-access television station carries a news program that is updated once or twice each week. Make sure you know the schedule of the local cable news

SAMPLE PRESS RELEASE

January 11, 2008
For Immediate Release
Contact: Jaimie Rosenthal
888-555-4758
Barrier-Free Coalition Presents to School Committee

The Barrier-Free Coalition of Madison High School will make a presentation before the Madison District School Committee at its next meeting, which starts at 7:30 p.m. on Thursday, January 19, 2008, in the Madison High School Library. The coalition's presentation will be made during the "Comments from the Community" period held at the start of each meeting.

The Barrier-Free Coalition is made up of students and faculty at Madison High School. The Coalition was formed when several students with physical disabilities started a dialogue about their difficulties navigating the high school. The high school, which was built in 1929, is listed as an historical property in the National Register. However, its narrow corridors, steep steps, and lack of elevators make getting around the school difficult, if not impossible, for many students.

"We have spoken with the high school principal about this issue, and she referred us to the School Committee," said Jaimie Rosenthal, spokesperson for the Coalition. "We spoke informally with members of the committee, who told us that there is no money in the school budget to make the school barrier free. So, we have come up with several possible low-cost solutions to help out short-term. We also have several ideas that could help to accomplish our goal of having a barrier-free school by 2009."

The Coalition will provide the School Committee with a PowerPoint presentation, preliminary drawings, and a cost-benefit analysis to support their suggestions, Ms. Rosenthal said. Handouts of the Coalition's materials will be available to members of the community.

For more information, contact Jaimie Rosenthal at 888-555-4758.

program, and then schedule your press release to reach the reporters and producers in plenty of time to have your news included in the next broadcast.

It is important to follow up your press release with a phone call. Ask for the editor who handles your community and ask which reporter has been assigned to your story. Find out who will be attending your event and whether the reporter will bring a photographer or camera operator. Because of the large volume of press releases they receive, editors sometimes get overwhelmed by requests, so a phone call will remind the editor to assign your story. Try to have the person who makes the follow-up call be your spokesperson, who can answer questions the editor or reporter may ask. If another person makes the calls, be sure that person refers all questions to your spokesperson.

AT YOUR EVENT

If you are making a presentation before a decision-making authority, be sure that your presentation is organized, clear, full of facts, brief, and closes with a proposed short-term or long-term solution or both. When it's possible and appropriate, have photos, graphs, and charts that illustrate your issue to present to the group and the audience attending the meeting. When your presentation is over, any reporters who attend may want to ask follow-up questions of your spokesperson. Be sure your spokesperson is aware of and has studied the facts, examples, laws, and other pieces of information he or she will need to make the presentation effective. It is always a good idea to rehearse before your presentation or event. Include follow-up questions in your rehearsal.

If you are scheduling a press conference, the spokesperson should start with a statement of the issue and its effects on you and/or your group, what you have done to try to find a resolution, and why you are now trying to seek public support for a resolution. A similar statement should be made at a demonstration or picketing place. Once the statement has been made, reporters who attend will ask questions to expand their story about your event. The spokesperson should be

Make plenty of copies of your statement and your graphics to give out to the board members and to the people attending your event. Put together packets of this information to give to the reporters who show up to cover your event.

The more work you do for the reporters who cover your presentation or event, the more likely it is that the coverage will be accurate. It is also more likely that the story about your issue will contain more facts and make a bigger impact on the public. The news media today operates with a small number of staff members who must cover many stories at once; you do yourself and your issue a favor by spending a little extra time to provide reporters with facts to support your goals.

careful to stick to the message you have decided on and not go off on tangents. Again, photos, graphs, illustrations, and charts are helpful, and copies of your material should be distributed.

Be aware that once the reporters, microphones, and cameras leave, you have no further control of what happens to your story. When you turn on the evening news or read the next day's paper, don't expect to read a verbatim repeat of what you said at your event. Good reporters will call "the other side" to do what's called a "reality check" on the information you provided at your event and to get another view of the story. Good reporters will be careful to avoid the appearance of siding with one group or another. Good reporters will be accurate, and try to convey, to the best of their ability, in the time or space they are allowed, what the issues are that face both you and the decision-making authority.

Even good reporters are overworked, and like all humans, can make mistakes. Not all reporters are as careful about details and accuracy as they should be. That is why we say it is important to be clear in all your statements and to distribute background material, including a copy of the statement your spokesperson makes. And that is why we advise coming up with a message and sticking to it.

DEVELOPING A MESSAGE— AND STICKING WITH IT

A message is the best tool to explain to the media (and the public) what your issue is all about and what your goal is. The words you use in your message should describe your situation and its preferred resolution in as few words as possible. Putting together a message forces you to think clearly in words that are easily understood. Having a message keeps you focused, especially when you are faced with a crisis. In a sound-bite world, having a message keeps you from saying the "wrong thing"—the thing that everyone will quote.

How to Develop a Message

◎ Narrow down the facts about your issue to a few most important points.

◎ Make a list of those points, then number them in order of priority.

◎ Choose three points to focus on—if you have a hard time narrowing it down to the three most important, choose one more, but don't have more than four points. These are called "talking points."

◎ For each of your points, come up with a sentence or two that explains it, choosing key words that in a simple but effective way reinforce your position.

◎ For each of your points, come up with a response to an objection a person or group might make against it (see chapter 2).

◎ Make a message box or triangle with your points.

◎ Practice answering a question from a reporter using your messages. Practice ways to get back to your message if a question leads you away from your main points.

Remember, you don't have to use message boxes if you find them too confusing!

USING MESSAGE BOXES

Message boxes are a tool you can use to help you focus when talking to the media. Many people who deal with the media on a regular basis have found that using message boxes helps them keep track of the things they want to say about their issue, and message boxes help avoid saying things that might be misunderstood. As newsmakers have discovered, it's a guarantee with the media: Once you go "off message," that's the quote the reporter will use!

So, try out the message box format to see if it works for you when dealing with the media (and others outside your organization) in your self-advocacy project:

- Use message boxes to organize the message points you have developed about your issue or program in a clear, concise format.
- Never try to use more than four main message points—three is better. When creating message boxes, use a triangle shape for three points, a box shape for four points.
- Start with a simple box or triangle form.
- In a message box, the most important point is at the top, the second is at the right, the third is at the bottom, and the fourth is at the left.
- In a message triangle, the message point at the right side of the triangle is the first and most important point. The second point is at the bottom; the third is at the left.
- Treat the message box as a focal point for your conversation with the press, always returning to the messages you have developed to underscore your position.

Using message points and message boxes may seem difficult and artificial at first, but it is worth it to practice: For example, come up with sample questions that the press might ask, and familiarize yourself with using the message points and message boxes in your answers. You will find that as you become used to them, you will feel uncomfortable without them. Why? Because they work!

SAMPLE MESSAGE BOXES

Your Main Message: We need barrier-free schools!
   Your Message Points:

- Barriers break the law.
- Barriers keep students from getting a good education.
- Without barriers, we can all be equal.
- Eliminating barriers now is cheaper in the long run.

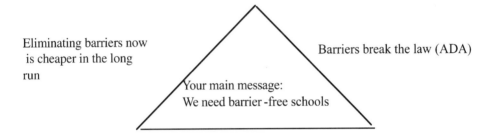

Barriers break the law (ADA)

Eliminating barriers now is cheaper in the long run

Your main message:
We need barrier -free schools

Barriers keep kids from getting a good education

Without barriers, we can all be equal

Eliminating barriers now is cheaper in the long run

Barriers break the law (ADA)

Your main message:
We need barrier -free schools

Without barriers, we can all be equal

Sample message boxes.

The most important thing when talking with the media is to get your message across to the public because you want the public to support your self-advocacy effort. The best way to do this is to stay with your message by using your "talking points." It doesn't matter if you sound like "a broken record." Your job in talking to the media is making sure that the public knows what your message is!

WHAT TO DO IF THE MEDIA MAKES A MISTAKE

It is difficult to get electronic media to make corrections—most television and radio stations aren't equipped to do so. If the mistake is a big one—for example, if the reporter gets your issue and goals completely wrong—it's important to call the reporter and then his editor or news director at the station, and firmly but politely ask for a correction. In some cases, the station will run a correction but be prepared that it will be short.

If the mistake or distortion of your views was in a newspaper, however, you have more options. Newspapers usually have an area of the publication where they correct mistakes—often on the bottom of page 2. So, when you contact the editor to tell him or her about the mistake, the correct information will probably be printed in that spot. Because it's hard to know how many people pay attention to corrections, it's a wise idea to also write a letter to the editor or an op-ed that briefly describes the error and your actual message about your issue. Letters are a widely read section of every newspaper, so readers are more likely to see and understand your actual message if you send the correction in letter format.

Message boxes are for your eyes only! When speaking with the press, answer each question clearly, incorporating the appropriate message point. But never show your message boxes to the media! They are a tool just for you and the rest of the people working with you on your self-advocacy project.

RELAX!

If you remember these basic points, your dealings with the media should go smoothly: The media is not your enemy; the media is not your friend; always stay on message when you talk to the media; and be prepared to "do reporters' work for them." Practice makes perfect—after a few experiences dealing with the media, you'll feel like an expert!

RESOURCE

Student Press Law Center
1101 Wilson Boulevard Suite 1100
Arlington, VA 22209
www.splc.org
703-807-1904

4 Personal Rights

Simply stated, personal rights are those that affect your person—that is, you and your body, including your physical and emotional well-being. Personal rights include your right to be safe and treated with respect at home, at school, at your job, and in the wider world. Personal rights also include your right to make choices that affect your well-being. Personal rights are not always easy to define or easy to make others understand because they are all connected with other issues you encounter just by being a teenager. For example:

- If you apply for a job and don't get it, can you tell for sure whether you didn't get the job because you are black or Hispanic or Jewish or female or because you don't have the skills the job requires?

- If you are denied privileges or are punished at home, can you tell if you're being disciplined because you are a teen and your parents are having a bad day or because you proved to be irresponsible in the past?

- If you are frisked at a bus station or an airport or pulled over when you're driving, can you know if you are being singled out because of the way you look or because you were the passenger or driver who was next in line in a system of random checks?

- If you have an encounter with law enforcement officials, do you believe that you are treated differently because you are a teenager, because you are a member of a minority group, or because of your behavior?

Unfortunately, many people in authority believe it is okay to discriminate against teenagers because they believe teens do not have the power to stand up for themselves if they are treated unfairly, illegally, or immorally.

Questions about personal rights don't always have easy answers. By using the steps outlined in chapter 2, however, you can decide whether your situation is one that calls for action and advocacy and then how to go about proceeding with a self-advocacy plan. You can avoid being a victim and put yourself in a position of power by knowing the issues, knowing your rights, and making your case as rationally and comprehensively as possible. This chapter gives you specific information about your personal rights and the laws that apply to your situation. It shows you the U.S. Supreme Court cases that have influenced how your rights are viewed. It shows you how to file a complaint if you believe your rights have been violated. It also lists places where you can find assistance in dealing with issues that arise in defense of your rights.

WHAT'S HAPPENING TO YOU?

Being a teenager is not a handicap or a disability. It is a fact of life! Not only that, every adult you meet has been where you are and has faced issues like the ones you face. Despite that, not all adults have the ability to put themselves in the position of a teen living in today's world. Potential employers, teachers and school administrators, law enforcement officials, and your parents may judge you based on their memories of their own youth rather than on who you are today. Although they were all teenagers at one time, they may remember only their experiences when they were your age or remember them in a romanticized way, and they may have expectations of you based on what they recall of their own situations when they were young. But there is no "one size fits all" for teenagers.

If you are reading this book, you have identified that you have an issue that needs to be addressed, and you don't want to be seen as just part of a group. Life has changed dramatically since the adults of today were teenagers. You are the one who is the most aware of the pressures in your life, what is going on around you, and what you need to succeed in life. You want to be seen as an individual and judged on your own strengths and abilities. Your individuality as a person is just as important as your age, your religion, or your race. Whenever you believe it is time to speak up for yourself, it is important to let people know that you are aware of who you are as a person.

WHAT DO PERSONAL RIGHTS MEAN TO YOU?

According to the laws of the United States, you are considered an adult at age eighteen. When you turn eighteen, you become an adult legally, but not all adults will see you as "one of them." However, the Supreme Court has decided that the rights granted in the Constitution and in the Bill of Rights also apply to teens (see the cases discussed in chapter 1). The hard part is persuading others to see teens like you as people with rights.

If you believe that you are being judged as a member of a group rather than as an individual, your personal rights may be violated. You may be the victim of profiling. According to the Amnesty International website, "Racial profiling occurs when race is used by law enforcement or private security officials, to any degree, as a basis for criminal suspicion in non-suspect specific investigations" (from www.amnestyusa.org/racial_profiling/index.do).

A broader definition of profiling is needed for the purpose of this chapter and would include using race, religion, national origin, age, or any other category when judging a person's actions or abilities. If you think that you are the victim of profiling in your search for a job or a place to live, your application to college, your dealings with the law, or even in social situations, you do have options. Discrimination based on these categories diminishes the human rights of *all* individuals and must not be tolerated.

WHAT ARE YOUR RIGHTS?

On December 10, 1948, the General Assembly of the United Nations (UN) adopted a Universal Declaration of Human Rights (UDHR). The declaration, which is similar to the U.S.

"The college admissions process at my high school became divided among racial lines. For example, the option of applying early admission to schools only was offered to white students. There were many black students from Newark who could have turned in their applications early, but the option was never encouraged, let alone mentioned.

The school headmaster told me that I would never get into Princeton. To advocate for myself, I reached out to parents of my friends and one of them set up a meeting for me with a Princeton professor who encouraged me to apply to the school. Once I got in to Princeton, I put up about 200 copies of my acceptance letter throughout the school. This not only allowed me to show certain individuals that their assumptions were wrong but also allowed me to help inspire students behind me. Advocating for oneself is extremely important not only for oneself but for the people around you."—Randy W.

Constitution, states, "Everyone is entitled to all the rights and freedoms set forth in this Declaration, without distinction of any kind, such as race, colour, sex, language, religion, political or other opinion, national or social origin, property, birth or other status." The rights covered by the declaration include the basic rights of life, liberty, and security of person, as well as the right to an education, to participate in cultural life, freedom from torture or cruel and inhuman treatment, and freedom of thought, conscience, and religion.

The assembly realized that to have peace, justice, and freedom in the world, all people need to be treated with respect and dignity. Human Rights Day is celebrated every year on December 10 to remind the world that "All human beings are

Dena al-Atassi is the daughter of a Syrian father and an American mother. Dena lived in Syria from the time she was fourteen until she returned to the United States in 2002 at seventeen. While in Syria, she studied Islam and began wearing a head scarf and long trench coat. As a result of harassment at the airport, she stopped wearing the scarf when she returned to the United States.

Dena kept her scarf off for eight months but was not comfortable going without it. She went to school at the University

Dena al-Atassi.

of Central Florida, where she was sought out because of her knowledge of Islam. Her professors asked Dena to speak in their classes to help raise awareness about Islam. She began to wear her head scarf again and got involved in a campaign against anti-Muslim stereotypes.

Dena is chairwoman of the Florida chapter of the Muslim Students Association at her university. She is using her position there to encourage other Muslims to advocate for their rights and to continue to help raise awareness about Islam and the plight of Muslims throughout the country and the world.

born with equal and inalienable rights and fundamental freedoms." In 1968, the UN General Assembly affirmed that the declaration was an obligation on the part of member nations to preserve and protect the rights of their citizens.

The UN Declaration is not a law that is enforceable. However, it is a powerful reference if you are advocating for your rights based on other laws that are enforceable. The full text of the law can be found online at www.un.org/Overview/rights.html. The United States federal law that covers discrimination against people because of race, color, religion, or national origin is the Civil Rights Act of 1964. The Civil Rights Act deals with the following rights: voting rights; treatment in any place of public accommodation; public education; federally assisted programs; and employment. The law also tells you how to file a complaint if you believe you have been discriminated against. Title II of the Civil Rights Act deals with public places, such as movie theaters, concerts, restaurants, and hotels. If a case is brought against an establishment under this section of the law, the Attorney General of the United States could intervene.

Title VII of the Civil Rights Act is enforced by the U. S. Equal Employment Opportunity Commission (EEOC) and protects you against discrimination in the workplace. Title VII only applies to people who hire fifteen or more employees and to state, local, and federal governments. The law applies to all aspects of the job, including hiring, firing, promotion, wages, and job training. This law does not include the corner bookstore or video game store where you might want to work part-time if it does not have fifteen or more employees. Still, the store's owners must certainly be aware of the EEOC and know that it is good business practice to follow the guidelines of the Civil Rights Act.

Affirmative action, that is, giving consideration to minorities by increasing recruitment and training in employment and by removing barriers to higher education, is a policy that has been implemented in many places to try to make up for past discrimination. If you are part of a minority group that has been discriminated against, you are likely to be helped by affirmative action policies. These policies are in place in the federal government, large and small corporations and businesses, and colleges and universities.

Regents of University of California v. Bakke (1978) is the Supreme Court case that dealt with civil rights and affirmative action regarding college admissions. There was no clear-cut decision in this case. Five Supreme Court justices ruled that a racial quota violated the Civil Rights Act of 1964 and that the white student involved in the case could not be denied admission. Four justices, however, said that it was permissible to use race as a criterion for admission to higher education. However, one of the five justices who ruled with the majority also sided with the other four justices in writing the minority opinion! As a result, minorities felt that the decision resulted in gains for them in regard to affirmative action. In *Gratz v. Bollinger* (2003), the Supreme Court upheld the policy of using race as a factor in determining admission to higher education.

When you are dealing with law enforcement officers, your rights are covered by the U. S. Constitution's Bill of Rights. In cases of this nature, it is important to know what your rights are so that you don't get into more trouble for breaking the law. If you are contacted by the police or other law enforcement agencies, it is always important to remember that you have the right to remain silent, you have the right to a lawyer, and you do not have to let officers search your home without a search warrant. If you are stopped on the street, you can ask if you are free to go. If law enforcement officers detain you (you are not under arrest, but you are not free to go), they can pat you down to see if you are armed or dangerous. You may have to give your name, but you do not have to answer other questions. If you are stopped in your car, civil rights attorneys suggest the following:

- ◎ **Keep your hands where the police can see them.**
- ◎ **You are not required to allow police to search your car, but they can do so if they have probable cause to believe you were involved in a crime or to believe you have evidence of a crime in your car.**
- ◎ **Clearly state that you do not consent to a search, but don't argue with the officers, and state your objections politely. Do not provoke an argument by being confrontational.**
- ◎ **Get the names and badge numbers, squad card number, and license plate number of the officers who stopped you. Make a note of the location and the time of day you were stopped. As soon as possible, write down what happened while it is fresh in your mind.**
- ◎ **If you believe that you have been mistreated, contract your local civil rights organization for legal advice.**

See chapter 9 for more information on dealing with the law.

WHERE AND HOW TO START

Filing a civil rights complaint or a complaint with the EEOC is a major step and should take place after careful consideration and after other remedies have failed. If you believe you have been discriminated against, talk with the employer, retail store or theater owner, or school guidance counselor involved to make sure your observations are correct. If you proceed with filing a complaint, check into the history of the school, business, or public site to see if it has a practice of this type of discrimination. If you have a case, you might be able to get together with others who have experienced the same type of discrimination. The presence of this type of history could make your case stronger. Once you decide on a path, carefully review the steps in chapter 2 before you begin.

WHERE ELSE TO GO

If you are still in school, there are many possible sources of advice. The school nurse, your guidance counselor, or a crisis management person at your school is used to dealing with the issues you are facing. You might also want to approach a favorite teacher at your school. These professionals are trained to talk with teenagers; they can help you see your options and guide you in the right direction. If you ask, school professionals will respect your confidentiality, except in cases where they are legally bound to

> "Don't go into an environment thinking that people will attack you. Go with a positive attitude and don't expect that you will be discriminated against. [Otherwise you] will be looking at every word and look [from people around you] as something negative. But be ready to protect yourself mentally and physically."—Manal, Palestinian/Muslim High School Student

report what you say. If that is a concern for you, you might first check out the reporting regulations that apply to your situation before starting a conversation.

It is important to realize that not all adult advice is good advice. Some adults may not be comfortable with your issues, and their advice and suggestions may reflect that. In addition, by their attitude they may make you feel that your issues are not important. Don't let that keep you from going after your goal. Just say "thank you" and move on. Bounce their ideas off others. Keep trying until you get what you need.

If you are wondering if the advice you receive from adults is helpful, ask others questions about the adults you have contacted and the advice they have given to you. You can often tell if adult advice is bad advice. Just ask these questions of yourself as you decide whether to accept the advice or not:

- Does the advice feel right?
- Does the adult listen to you?
- What is the adult's approach?
- Does the adult appear threatened by you?

Check with your local civil rights agencies. If there is a local chapter of the American Civil Liberties Union (ACLU) in your town, contact them. The ACLU has divisions that are solely dedicated to the rights of teenagers, and the organization is concerned about issues of discrimination. The ACLU can also give you legal advice and help you file a complaint. The national office is located at 125 Broad Street, Eighteenth Floor, New York, NY 10004. You can find local offices through the ACLU website at www.aclu.org.

EMPLOYMENT

If you believe your employment rights have been violated due to discrimination, you can file a complaint with the EEOC. Every district has its own office, and you are required to file through the office in your area. Check your phone book or look the EEOC up online at www.eeoc.gov/offices.html. You will need specific information to file a discrimination claim, and the EEOC can tell you what you need. The EEOC national address is:

U.S. Equal Employment Opportunity Commission
1801 L Street, N.W.
Washington, D.C. 20507
Phone: (202) 663-4900
TTY: (202) 663-4494

PERSONAL RESPONSIBILITY, PERSONAL NEEDS AND WANTS

This chapter is concerned primarily with advocating for your personal rights, that is, those that are guaranteed to you by the U. S. Constitution and its amendments. However, self-advocacy is also important in attaining your personal needs and wants, that is, the things you want to accomplish while you are a teen and in your life, including the personal freedoms you would like to have. Self-advocacy is also critical in situations where you need to resist peer pressure to avoid a risky activity that could result in physical or emotional harm to you.

Self-advocacy can make the difference in whether or not you achieve your personal goals, whether your goals are as simple as getting permission to drive your family car, as complicated as getting into the college you want to attend, or as important as finding the right job to support yourself or to further your career. In many ways, being a successful self-advocate for your personal wants and needs means taking personal responsibility for your attitude, your speech, your actions, and even your attire. That's especially the case when you are faced with an opportunity to do something risky and you want to resist peer pressure.

A group of teenagers in California turned a class project into getting a bill passed into law in their state. The class project originally involved finding the reasons for Marin County's high rate of breast cancer. The teens became aware of potential health risks in the ingredients used to make cosmetic products they used on a regular basis. They discovered that some of the ingredients were linked to cancer. For example, through laboratory research, acrylamide, an ingredient in many foundations, face lotions, and hand creams, has been linked to mammary tumors. Dibutyl phthalate, a chemical in many perfumes and hair sprays, has been linked to an increase in breast cancer. The teens also learned that the U.S. Food and Drug Administration (FDA) is not required to test cosmetic ingredients for safety.

The group began to call itself Teens for Safe Cosmetics. They lobbied at the state capital and tried to see and talk with the state governor. The teens were allowed to make their case, and their efforts resulted in a bill, SB 484, which was passed and signed into law by the governor in 2005. The law requires cosmetics manufacturers to disclose, in ads and on labels, potentially cancer-causing ingredients in their products. The law also authorizes California's Department of Health Services to research the effects of chemicals in cosmetics that might be linked to cancer or birth defects and to submit its findings to other state agencies. Manufacturers that do not make that information available are violating the law. Teens for Safe Cosmetics saw that, even though they were not old enough to vote, they had the power to effect change in something important to their daily lives.

Let's say you want an after-school job at your local bookstore. You've seen a sign in the window that says "Part-time Help Wanted." In the first scenario, you could just drop in at the store after soccer practice one day dressed in cutoffs and a tank top and ask for the job on the spot. In the second scenario, you could do some research and be prepared to present yourself at your best:

- If you shop at the store regularly, get an idea of how the store is staffed, how the store is organized, and whether the owner or manager is usually at the store.

⑨ **Call the owner or manager and set up an appointment to meet at a specific time.**

⑨ **Be sure you are freshly showered and dressed in clean clothes that are appropriate for business, not for the beach, and arrive on time or a little early for the appointment.**

⑨ **Tell the manager or owner that you love books and reading and are always on the lookout for the latest books. Be sure that is true, and be sure that you are familiar with authors and titles popular with your age group.**

⑨ **Make it clear that you're familiar with the store and know how it is set up.**

⑨ **Give the owner or manager a simple resume, that is, a sheet of paper that provides your name, address, and phone number, your grade in school, a list of places you've worked or volunteered before, and a list of two or three references. (References should be adults who know you well, other than your family members, including teachers, former employers, your clergyperson, or a coach. Always ask permission before you use a person's name for a reference.)**

In which scenario do you think it's more likely that you will be offered a job? In the second scenario, you have taken the personal responsibility to advocate for yourself by doing your research, knowing your audience, and following the other steps detailed in chapter 2.

The basic steps outlined in chapter 2 can be adapted to use whether you are looking for a job or seeking another personal want or need. The steps are essential, for example, if you want to demonstrate that you are mature enough to handle additional responsibility at home, especially if you need to reestablish trust after breaking a rule. The steps are particularly useful when applying to college or to get into an elite program that is important to you.

PEER PRESSURE

Most of the time, going along with the crowd is enjoyable. It is fun to study with friends, to volunteer at community service activities, or to try out new ideas with people your own age.

Teens on Target (TNT) is an example of how teens working together can change policies that affect their lives. TNT is a youth violence prevention program started in Oakland, California, in 1989 in response to shootings in schools. The purpose was to train teenagers to advocate solutions to violence. In 1991, the members worked on a project to reduce the number of guns being sold in their area as a way to limit the violence. They felt it was too easy for young people to get guns and that was one of the major causes of the youth violence in their communities. The teens gathered evidence in the form of video and audio recordings of the sounds in their neighborhoods at night—weapons firing, ambulance sirens, etc.—and personal stories of friends and family members who had been killed or injured and presented this to the Oakland City Council at a public hearing. The city council responded to the presentation and passed a resolution against residential gun dealers.

Sometimes, however, going along can be dangerous, if your friends are involved in illegal or risky behaviors and try to get you involved. The risks can vary from distracting you from your schoolwork to getting you injured or arrested.

Peer pressure can be powerful. Most teens want to fit in and don't want to disappoint their friends. You may be asked to show your loyalty by taking part in an activity along with the rest of your friends. It may seem like fun at the moment to cheat in school; skip class; use alcohol, tobacco, or illegal drugs; go somewhere or be with someone that your parents do not approve of; or drive too fast.

If you are like most teens, you probably don't believe that bad things can happen to you. You think that the chances of getting hurt or getting caught when you do something risky are small. Think about it rationally. You already might have lost a friend in a car accident, to violence on the street, or because he or she went along with a risky behavior after having too much alcohol to drink. According to the National Institute of Alcohol Abuse and Alcoholism, each year approximately five thousand youths under age twenty-one die as a result of underage drinking. This includes those who die in car accidents, homicides, suicides, and through other injuries, such as falling, burning, and drowning.

There are no laws that will protect you from peer pressure. What will protect you is using common sense and advocating for yourself. You can use some of the tips in chapter 2 to advocate for your well-being with your peers at school. The United States Department of Health and Human Services suggests the following steps to help you make an informed decision about a risky activity suggested by your friends:

- **Identify what needs to be decided.**
- **Gather the information necessary to make the decision— including possible solutions or alternatives. One choice may involve fitting in with the crowd, breaking the law, and risking damage to your young body and brain. Another choice may involve thinking of other ways to have fun with friends and still be popular, avoid harm, and stick to your family's values.**
- **List the possible courses of action. You can do this in your head!**
- **Think about the consequences of poor choices: disappointing Mom and Dad, getting grounded, being involved in a possible car crash, or having unwanted sex.**
- **Healthy choices may lead to taking pride in a healthy outlook, staying safe, and realizing that you alone—not your peers—will live with the results of your choices.**
- **Make a decision: for example, you might decide not to use alcohol until age twenty-one.**
- **Review and reinforce with yourself that you can make your own choices, that you have the courage to say *no* when something your friends want to do conflicts with your values, and that you can be true to yourself.**
- **Practice using these decision-making skills so that they feel automatic when a choice arises. That way, you won't have to make an on-the-spot decision that could result in bad choices.**

Take personal responsibility for achieving your goals, and self-advocate. If you always do your research, know your audience, choose the right time to make your case, then have a backup plan for negotiation, your rate of success will multiply!

MORE RESOURCES FOR HELP

Amnesty International is a worldwide organization that focuses on preventing abuses to rights and ending discrimination. Its main office is at:

Amnesty International USA
5 Penn Plaza, 16th Floor
New York, N.Y. 10001
www.amnestyusa.org
Tel: 212-807-8400
Fax: 212-627-1451
1-800-AMNESTY

There are many national and international agencies that provide legal help to teenagers. Check the Internet or your phone book to find local legal aid societies in your area. There are also many Internet sites that give advice to teens on a variety of topics. You need to make sure the advice and support is right for you. Question any advice given by people you don't know— that is, question it even more closely than you would question advice given face-to-face. Make sure that the advice feels right to you and that there are no expectations that you will do something in exchange for the advice. Check out the motivation of the advice giver. Is the person concerned about your individual interests, or is he or she promoting a different agenda? Is it possible that the people or groups would like to take advantage of your situation to accomplish their goals? If any of these is the case, your situation could become worse than it is. Again, go with your gut!

5 School Issues

Most of your day-to-day expectations in school are fairly ordinary. You want to make sure you can get to school, get to your classes, and learn in a safe and secure atmosphere. You want time to be with your friends at lunch and between classes. You want to feel respected by your friends, teachers, and administrators. You want to feel that you have some control over your education and your future.

A situation at a high school in the Bronx, New York, at the beginning of the 2005–2006 school year showed that ordinary expectations are not always fulfilled or easy to come by. Before school opened in September, metal detectors were installed at the high school entrances to make sure that students were safe and secure. The students had to line up, remove metal from their pockets, take off any metal they were wearing, and have their book bags searched. Of course, safety is an important goal and is a basic expectation to have in your school. However, in the Bronx, it took so much time for all students to pass through the metal detectors that students were often late to class. They were no longer able to leave the building at lunchtime because it took too much time to pass students through the metal detectors and into the building for a second time.

The students at the school became frustrated, and finally, many of them decided to do something about the situation. The students' self-advocacy project began with one student asking others to join him on a particular day outside the school to protest the new security situation. The group of students swelled to fifteen hundred. Seeing the strength of their numbers,

High school. Photo by Ross Tuttle.

the students decided on the spot to walk two miles to the office of the Department of Education to voice their concerns. Four of the students were eventually asked into the office, where they presented their group's concerns. They explained how students were feeling about the metal detectors and lunch restrictions and their concerns about a previous ban on cell phones. The officials at the department agreed to keep listening to students' concerns and negotiating with students.

As a result of the students' action on their own behalf, more metal detectors were installed at the high school to keep entrance lines down. In addition, a group of students started working with counselors at the school to draw up a written document about the issues that spurred student action, in an effort to determine how changes could be made in the way decisions are implemented at the school. Moreover, the school sponsored an all-day assembly on activism to support the courage of the protesting students and to help them learn how to channel their advocacy energy in positive ways for personal issues, school issues, and in the wider world. An idea that began with one student is having far-reaching results for the rest of the students at the school.

Situations arise at schools on an ongoing basis in which students are at odds with the school's administration. In many cases, both students and the administration believe they know best regarding discipline, zero tolerance, dress codes, drug testing, free speech and expression, privacy, and off-campus conduct. The reality is that there are rules in every school mandating what is acceptable and what is not. Even though there may have been student input into developing those rules, you may not agree with them. As the students in the Bronx showed, disagreeing with school policy is not always a take-it-or-leave-it proposition. There are ways to make your preferences known, and even if you can't change the rules, you might find a way to reach a compromise that feels more comfortable to you. Or you can begin a dialogue for future consideration.

If you believe that there is a good reason to protest the rules and regulations at your school, it is important to know your rights, to develop goals, and to use self-advocacy skills to achieve those goals.

In this chapter, we discuss U.S. Supreme Court cases that have been decided about what schools can do in regard to discipline, speech, searches, and due process, how peer pressure can be a major factor in your behavior at school, and how you can advocate for yourself with the school administration.

WHAT'S HAPPENING TO YOU?

As stated in chapter 1, rights for teens began to be taken seriously in the 1960s, but those rights are not absolute. The rights of students inside a school (or in a school-sponsored or school-related activity outside of school) are not the same as those for adults. There are many different ways to interpret the law as it applies to teenagers in a school setting. The good news is that interpretations of these laws are not arbitrary. Most of the time, they are based on cases that either have come before the U.S. Supreme Court or before lower courts in individual states. The not-so-good news, for teens who disagree with their school's rules, is that most major cases have been decided in favor of the schools. The language used in the decisions justifies the limits placed on students' rights, that is, as those rights relate to constitutional amendments.

There have been many cases heard in federal and state courts since the 1960s regarding the rights of students. We have selected five major cases: *Tinker v. Des Moines Independent School District* (1968), *Goss v. Lopez* (1975), *New Jersey v. T.L.O.* (1985), *Bethel School District No. 403 v. Fraser* (1986), and *Hazelwood School District v. Kuhlmeier* (1988). The Supreme Court justices referred to previous decisions to help them determine the outcome of these five.

In *Tinker v. Des Moines Independent School District*, the Supreme Court ruled that First Amendment guarantees of free speech apply to students and that what a student wears can be considered "pure speech." In *Tinker*, students were suspended from school for wearing black armbands to protest the Vietnam War. The court held that the students' right to wear the armbands was protected by the First Amendment because the action was an expression of their political opinion and would not substantially interfere with school discipline.

In *Goss v. Lopez*, the issue was one of due process rights guaranteed under the Fourteenth Amendment. Nine students were suspended from a high school in Ohio for ten days because of a disturbance in the lunchroom that damaged school property. One of the students, Dwight Lopez, denied that he was involved, but he was refused a hearing. No hearings were held before the suspensions were ordered. The students and their parents fought the suspensions in court, and the case eventually ended up before the U.S. Supreme Court. The high court ruled that the school could not take away a student's right to an education without prior notice and without a hearing to determine if, in fact, the action they were disciplined for actually took place.

In *New Jersey v. T.L.O.*, a student was accused of smoking in the girl's bathroom. While she was being questioned, her purse was searched, drug paraphernalia was found in her purse, and she was charged with delinquency. The student tried to have the evidence (and her confession to selling marijuana at school) thrown out on the grounds that the search was unlawful. The Supreme Court stated that a school could use a less strict standard when searching a student's possessions and that the search did not violate the Fourth or Fourteenth Amendments. The high court said that the search was reasonable because the school officials had reasonable grounds to suspect that the search would show evidence that the student had violated school rules.

In *Bethel School District No. 403 v. Fraser*, the court found that it was appropriate for a school to prohibit vulgar and offensive language in a speech delivered at school. A student was suspended for using graphic sexual metaphors in his nominating speech for a friend at a school assembly. He appealed the action, and the U.S. Supreme Court eventually heard the case. The high court decided that the student's First Amendment rights were not violated because the school can prohibit vulgar and offensive language that is not consistent with the fundamentals of school education, and the high court said that the determination of what type of speech is inappropriate rests with the school board.

In *Hazelwood School District v. Kuhlmeier*, a school principal refused to let students publish articles that he felt were inappropriate. The articles were to be published in a school-sponsored newspaper that was written and edited by the students of Hazelwood East High School in St. Louis County, Missouri. The prohibited articles had to do with teen pregnancy and the impact of divorce on young people. The students appealed the principal's action, and the case ended up in the U.S. Supreme Court. The high court ruled that the school had the right to set high standards for student speech (written articles in the school newspaper) set out by the school, and that the school could determine and prohibit speech that did not go along with the shared values of the school.

The cases cited here, and the underlying constitutional issues that most school complaints are based on are:

◎ **First Amendment: The right to freedom of expression,**

◎ **Fourth Amendment: Freedom from unreasonable searches, and**

◎ **Fourteenth Amendment: Due process (notification before you are disciplined).**

In most schools, students can be suspended from school for breaking school rules. An appeal of the rules will be viewed by the legal system based on what schools have done in the past, what the courts say schools can do, and whether students' constitutional rights appear to be violated.

FREEDOM OF EXPRESSION

Your freedom to express yourself in school is guaranteed by two constitutional amendments:

- **The First Amendment says that the government cannot abridge "the freedom of speech, or of the press; or the right of the people peaceably to assemble, and to petition the government for a redress of grievances."**
- **The Fourteenth Amendment gives you the right of sufficient notice of any policy that regulates your expression or penalizes your conduct and says that notice must be clear and to the point and given within enough time for you to change your conduct accordingly.**

Speech

Your freedom of expression is guaranteed by the First Amendment, but your school can establish rules against speech that they believe interferes with the school's educational process. In other words, the school can establish a rule against obscene language and profanity if administrators believe that use of that kind of language will interfere with the educational fundamentals being offered at the school.

For the most part, you cannot be punished for what you say just because the administrators at your school don't like what you say, unless your speech falls into the category of what is prohibited at your school. You cannot be disciplined for expressing your personal views on a subject unless the administrators feel that your expression will disrupt the work of the school or interfere with the rights of other students. School administrators do not have to wait to see if you cause a disruption if they can reasonably forecast that a disruption will result if you are allowed to express yourself in a certain way.

The school must, however, make sure that the rules of what is acceptable are clear and that you have sufficient notice about what is acceptable and what is not. If the terms are so vague that you have to guess at their meaning, it would be difficult for you to adhere to that rule. Look carefully at your school's rules about acceptable speech before challenging the authority.

Self-advocacy involves self-awareness and self-preservation. Remember the steps in chapter 2—especially the steps about research and knowing your audience. Your self-advocacy project will come to a screeching halt and do more harm than good if you choose to express yourself in language that explicitly violates school rules.

Dress Codes

Dress codes and rules about appropriate and inappropriate clothing are covered under the First Amendment free-speech clause, because speech can also mean conduct that communicates. This includes signals given in a baseball game as well as wearing a message printed on your T-shirt. The right to free expression, as it applies to what you wear, is not absolute. Although your choice of clothing can be protected under the Constitution as a form of self-expression, your school board can control what you wear if it believes that your choice would interfere with the rights of others. For example, the text or an image on your T-shirt may offend a religious or ethnic group, or it might be such a graphic image that it causes a distraction that would interfere with the work of the school. School systems have a right to regulate what you wear if they believe that keeping you from wearing something disruptive outweighs your right to free speech. The school can also institute a school uniform policy if the policy is mandated for reasons that further the purpose of the school, whether that purpose is improving discipline or test scores.

MICHAEL GETS TO WEAR SKIRTS

Michael Coviello, a high school senior in New Jersey, took his protest to a higher level. He had worn shorts to school for three years because of a knee injury and knee braces but was suspended from school when he wore shorts after the knee braces were removed. Since he had grown during those three years, he no longer had pants to wear. So, to start with, he wore Halloween costumes instead.

Michael Coviello

At that point, "I was told that I had to go home and get pants, which I didn't have, go to talk to the superintendent, or get suspended from school. So I went to the superintendent." In his discussion with the superintendent, Michael asked why girls didn't have to wear pants and could wear skirts that did not cover their legs. "The superintendent said I could wear a skirt. So I bought some skirts. I didn't buy pants because they were too uncomfortable after all this time and they couldn't give me a valid reason for doing so."

When Michael wore the skirts to school, even though the superintendent had given him permission to do so, the school principal accused him of trying to make a mockery of the school and would not allow him back in school if he didn't wear pants. At that point, Michael and his parents wrote a letter to the local American Civil Liberties Union (ACLU) and detailed all that had gone on. "We met with the lawyer at the ACLU in Newark, and she said she would be interested in working with us. The ACLU sent the superintendent a letter about the First Amendment constitutional rights that were being broken. The result was that my parents and I had a meeting with the school's attorney, the principal, the superintendent, and the ACLU lawyer."

At the end of the meeting, it was decided that Michael could wear skirts to school, but because of school policy, he still could not wear shorts except in the warmer months of school. The ACLU was satisfied with the result and considered it a victory. The board of education of Michael's school district had another vote after meeting with the ACLU to consider changing the shorts policy but did not reverse the policy.

Michael then used another advocacy strategy. "When I turned eighteen and they had the election for board of education members, I got my friends to vote and we voted in new board members." According to Michael, "The biggest reason I did it was that I wanted to stand up for what I believed in and I thought that was the most important thing I could do."

However, your school cannot ban an article of clothing or jewelry just because administrators don't like it or because it is controversial. A school system's clothing regulations must meet three criteria. The school system must be able to prove:

◎ **That the ruling does not suppress your ability to express yourself,**

◎ **That the ruling is in the interest of the school, and**

◎ **That the ruling does not prohibit more than is necessary in furthering their interests.**

All three of these conditions must be in place for a school to ban the use of certain clothing.

If you are considering protesting a ruling about clothing in your school, first consider if the school can prove its ruling does not violate your First Amendment rights. For example, if you want to wear a T-shirt supporting a political candidate or a position on a social issue, the school cannot prohibit you from wearing that shirt: if doing so would suppress your ability to state your opinion; if your T-shirt is not causing a disruption; if the ban does not extend to other T-shirts with similar types of messages; or if the ban keeps you from expressing your opinion in other ways, such as political buttons or writing articles for the school newspaper.

If you believe that your issue about freedom of speech can be argued based on these points, familiarize yourself with the laws so you can state them clearly in your argument and move ahead.

DUE PROCESS AND ZERO TOLERANCE

Corporal Punishment

Federal courts of appeal in five different locations have ruled that the Fourteenth Amendment protects students from corporal punishment. Excessive corporal punishment is a violation of the amendment if it is so brutal and harmful that it shocks the court's conscience. Punishment shocks the court's conscience if: It cannot be justified by a legitimate concern; the force is excessive under the circumstances; and there is serious danger that a student could be severely injured. In the issue of corporal punishment, states may adopt rules that are different from the federal guidelines, so it is important to know what your particular state says about corporal punishment before advocating for your rights in this area.

Suspensions and Expulsions

Suspensions and expulsions from school are guided by the due process clause of the Fourteenth Amendment. A suspension occurs when you are temporarily removed from school. An expulsion occurs when you are permanently removed from school. You can only be expelled or suspended from school for specific reasons and only in a way that satisfies the safeguards of that amendment. A suspension or expulsion is justified only if a student's behavior "materially and substantially" interferes with the operation of the school, or if the student presents a "clear and present danger of physical injury" to himself or herself, to other students, to adults, or to the property of the school. These criteria may also apply to behavior outside of

Schools have rules of conduct that all students must follow. Those rules should be provided, in writing, so that all students know what is expected and so that they know what behaviors will result in a suspension and what behavior will trigger an expulsion. Many schools now provide students with handbooks that explain rules of conduct—it's important that you obtain a copy of your school's handbook, if there is one, before embarking on a self-advocacy project.

school if that behavior makes it unsafe for the other students, teachers, or property of the school.

A school system must make every effort to address and defuse a behavior problem before suspending or expelling a student. Possible efforts the school system must make include counseling, parent conferences, behavior modification plans, or temporary changes in placement. If you are suspended or expelled, you are entitled to a hearing to discuss the charges, and you must be allowed to present your side of the story. The rules regarding this type of hearing vary from state to state. In some cases, you might want to be represented by a lawyer, or you might want to present witnesses or written testimonials from people who know you or who were at the scene of the alleged misbehavior. If the offense is related to searches or to something you have written or said, refer to the other sections in this chapter that deal with freedom of expression and privacy. Check your state's guidelines regulating suspensions and expulsions to make sure you have all the information you need to tell your side. See chapter 6 on how a determination of a learning disability affects suspension.

Zero Tolerance

Zero tolerance is a disciplinary method designed to protect you from other students who might be dangerous. Zero-tolerance policies are put in place for serious offenses, such as assaults with a weapon. Zero-tolerance policies may also be put in place for use when a school can prove that it is not possible or reasonable to have a hearing before removing a student from school. Zero tolerance provides for fast and easy removal of potentially dangerous students from the school population. Zero tolerance, in one form or another, is a rule in the majority of the schools in the United States.

If you believe you are in danger because of the actions of another student, zero tolerance is a policy that you might support. If you are the person being suspended from school as a result of an infraction covered by a zero-tolerance policy, you might have a different perspective. Good zero-tolerance policies

In 1999, Jennifer Boccia and fifteen other students at Allen High School in Allen, Texas, wore black armbands to school to protest new school policies implemented in response to the tragic Columbine High School shootings in Littleton, Colorado. They also wore the armbands in respect for the shooting victims. The students were aware of the 1969 Supreme Court decision *Tinker v. Des Moines Independent School District* that upheld students' rights to wear black armbands to protest the Vietnam War. Just like the students in the *Tinker* case, however, the three students in Texas were suspended when they refused school administrators' demand that they remove their armbands.

When she was suspended, Jennifer contacted the media and appeared on many local TV stations and in the newspaper. The school principal offered to clear her record if she stopped talking to the press, admitted that the school was right to suspend her, and agreed to follow school rules in the future. Jennifer did not accept the offer, and with the help of the ACLU of Texas, she filed a federal court lawsuit, *Boccia v. The Allen Independent School District*. The district agreed to settle the case in Jennifer's favor. The settlement states that Jennifer's suspension for wearing a black armband as a symbol of protest violated her First and Fourth Amendment rights. It also stated that the district's attempt to keep her from talking to the media violated Jennifer's free speech rights.

Diana Philip, Regional Director of the ACLU of Texas, said, "Our young people have the same rights to express sentiments that may disfavor school policies without fear of punishment, be it expressing views through a manner of protest without disrupting the educational environment or speaking to the media or public at large about issues important to them." Philip added, "These are the lessons we need to teach our kids in order to become productive citizens and respectful leaders in our communities."

allow for due process for any student accused of being a danger to the school. Due process for zero-tolerance policies makes sure that the discipline a student receives is administered fairly. Zero tolerance is a controversial issue and is not one with a quick and easy answer. If you think due process has been violated and you want to challenge a ruling, remember to weigh safety with your right to due process before filing a protest.

As the *Goss v. Lopez* case showed, you have a right to tell your side of the story before you are suspended as a disciplinary measure. As Dr. Martin Luther King Jr. once said, "Injustice anywhere threatens justice everywhere." Many people involved in school administration and students' rights believe that we should question whether the only way to preserve order in our schools is to suspend individual rights. See chapter 9 for more information about what you can do if you are charged with a zero-tolerance policy infraction.

Truancy

If you are under sixteen, you are required to attend school, unless you are in a homeschooling program that has been approved by the school system. If you fail to attend school for more than four days in a row without an excused absence, you may be considered truant. See chapter 9 for more information about truancy and how it can affect you.

Privacy

Searches

As the students in the Bronx discovered, schools have the right to search what you bring to school to make sure you are not bringing in anything that is unsafe to other students. When a school searches for weapons, it also has the ability to look at what else you bring in to the school. Schools have a right to do this because searches meet the conditions laid down by the law. The Fourth Amendment (amended) is not violated:

- If the school employee has reasonable grounds to suspect the search will turn up evidence that the student has violated the law or school rules; and
- If the conduct of the search is not too intrusive and is related to what they are looking for.

If all students are subjected to metal detectors, the search is considered not too intrusive, and it is allowed. If a handheld metal detector is waved over a student from an appropriate distance, that is also allowed. However, if students are touched by the person doing the search, if the handheld detector comes too close to the student's body, or if a student is required to take off personal clothing, the search could be a violation of personal rights. It's important to keep in mind that, even though your school has the right to search you, you do not surrender all your rights to privacy when you enter the school. You can reasonably appeal a search that you believe goes too far. (See chapter 9 for more information.)

Drug Testing

The practice of requiring high school athletes to undergo drug testing has been upheld in the courts. In some cases, the court has allowed students who participate in other competitive extracurricular activities also to be tested. However, the rationale for drug testing must show that there is reasonable suspicion that a real and immediate problem exists. If the group being tested has been involved with drugs in the past, it is reasonable to test the students in the group.

Drug testing programs cannot be used as a deterrent to future drug use and cannot be used to test all public school students. There have been rulings in many states about drug testing conducted in schools. In some cases, the school's testing program has been upheld; in others, the court ruled that students' rights were violated. The debate continues as school districts across the country consider whether they need to do random drug testing.

If you have a concern about drug testing in your school, it's important to question the rationale behind the policy. Determine whether the school's concerns meet the test of a reasonable suspicion of a real and immediate problem. If you or your parents have an opportunity to attend a hearing before a drug testing policy is implemented in your school, make sure you attend and that your views are heard. If you think that your rights were violated as a result of drug testing at your school, do your homework on this issue and advocate for your rights.

Off-Campus Conduct

When you are away from school at a school-sponsored activity, the rules and regulations that apply to you in school are still applicable. However, in some cases, you may have even fewer rights under the Fourth Amendment (against unreasonable searches) than when you are on school grounds. That is due to the increased responsibility of the staff when you are away from school. If searches that take place off school property are reasonable in their justification and their scope and are conducted by a school employee while you are away on a school-sponsored trip, the searches do not violate your Fourth Amendment rights. Your right to protest the reasonableness of the search is also the same as it would be if you were in school when the search occurred.

Your right to free speech may also not be the same when you are away from school and is not always guaranteed under the First Amendment. If what you say or write while off campus constitutes a "true threat," or if your off-campus behavior causes a substantial disruption or interference with school activities, your rights are not protected under the First Amendment—even if what you said or wrote was done in your home or at an off-campus activity. However, if your school disciplines you for something you said or did off campus (including websites you created at home), you have a right to appeal the disciplinary action. Before you appeal, however, be sure that the school violated these three principles:

- The school's decision must meet the test that what you did or said will disrupt the work of the school or interfere with the rights of other students;
- The rules regarding what is acceptable must be clear; and
- You were given sufficient notice about what is acceptable and what is not

Substance Abuse

You have certain rights when it comes to searching and testing for drugs and alcohol while you are in school or at off-campus activities. You also have responsibilities to yourself in regard to your substance use. Learn the law regarding alcohol and other drug use to make informed decisions for yourself.

There are many illegal substances available to teens, including alcohol, which you cannot legally purchase until age twenty-one. There are many people who have an interest in getting you to purchase and use illegal substances. Make sure you know the consequences for your actions. Your school might have a right to search your locker and backpack for drugs and alcohol. If substances are found, you could be suspended or expelled from school. The school may have the right to test you for drugs and alcohol in certain situations. Your school may have a policy about off-campus use of illegal substances that could result in your suspension or expulsion.

There are legal and health issues to substance use and abuse that can have long-term or even drastic effects on your health, limit your freedom, or interfere with your ability to work. In states that have a zero-tolerance policy for underage alcohol use, drinking one drink can cause you to fail a Breathalyzer test. Failing the test could mean that you lose your driver's license, be subject to heavy fines, or have your right to drive taken away permanently. Teen alcohol use can cause permanent brain damage. Drinking, especially binge drinking, could cause you to engage in risky behavior that can endanger your health and your life.

Club drugs (a wide variety of drugs often used at all-night dance parties ["raves"], nightclubs, and concerts), cocaine, hallucinogens, heroin, marijuana, methamphetamine, and steroids are illegal to buy and sell at any age. Like alcohol, use of these drugs can endanger your health and lead to high-risk behavior.

If you get involved with the law or the school as a result of your or your friend's drug or alcohol abuse, refer to chapter 9 for information about how to obtain legal help and how you can use your self-advocacy skills to your best advantage. See the section on peer pressure in chapter 4 to avoid getting into that position in the first place.

The United States Department of Health and Human Services has a clearinghouse with information that can help you if you believe you have a drug or alcohol problem:

SAMHSA's National Clearinghouse for Alcohol and Drug Information
800-729-6686
TDD 800-487-4889
linea gratis en español
877-767-8432

HOW DO SCHOOL ISSUES AFFECT YOU?

In 1969, in the decision on *Tinker v. Des Moines Independent School District*, Supreme Court Justice Abe Fortas stated in his majority opinion that "It can hardly be argued that either students or teachers shed their constitutional rights to freedom of speech or expression at the schoolhouse gate." You spend approximately half your waking hours in school or in school-related activities. What you learn in school is not limited to classroom work or the textbooks you read. You have rights and responsibilities as a student, and the adults at your school have rights and responsibilities. How the students, staff, and administration handle those rights and responsibilities is a lesson in democracy and a learning experience. The way issues are resolved in a school is similar to what goes on in U.S. society as a whole; what you do in school is a foundation for how you will live in society. As stated by the ACLU of New Jersey, in its publication *Students' Rights Handbook*, second edition, "It is the responsibility of students to be vigilant so that when civil liberties issues arise in school, they will be resolved in a way that respects constitutional principles" (p. 32).

WHAT ARE YOUR RIGHTS?

Ask yourself: Is what's happening to you or to your group morally, ethically, or legally wrong? Resolving an injustice in school does not need to become a confrontation. As stated in chapter 2, there are right ways and wrong ways to assert your rights. Sometimes, you only need to raise the awareness of those around you. Sometimes you may need to go further to resolve your issue. How you do that depends on the type of violation you have been accused of and your relationship with the staff and administration at your school. Your right to a free and appropriate public education also implies that the education is free from discrimination, free from restrictions on your speech and expression, free from search and seizure, and free from extreme discipline.

Eunice, a sophomore at a high school in New York, believed that she was being harassed because of a hat she wore at school. She wrote a letter to the editor of the school newspaper explaining her reasons for keeping her head covered. She told us "In my school newspaper, I describe an incident in which I was not even in the hallway or able to be seen from the door—which means the dean who did see me had to have made a note to himself to stop by my class to harass me. When the school newspaper was published, most of the questions and all of the harassment about my hat ended." In this case, simply drawing attention to the problem was enough to resolve the problem.

WHO HAS THE POWER TO HELP?

The first place to state your concerns at school is at the level closest to you. Teachers, guidance counselors, and school administrators are adults who have chosen to work with teenagers, and ideally, they have your interests at heart. However, you will not always feel comfortable with every one of your teachers, just as you don't choose to be friends with all the students at your school. Personality is an important factor in finding your comfort level with adults and other students. Some teachers are more tolerant than others, and some are easier to talk with. Start to discuss your concerns with someone who makes you feel the most comfortable. If you believe you need to go beyond your local school to protest a violation of your rights, review the steps outlined in chapter 2. There is a chain of command in every school bureaucracy, and you will need to learn the levels in your local district, city, or town. Call your local school committee or board of education administration office and ask where you should send a letter of protest or concern.

WHERE AND HOW TO START

Where and how to start your protest of a rights violation depends on how much time you have before the issue must be resolved. The students in the Bronx (discussed previously in this chapter) did not feel they had a lot of time to waste. They saw the school year progressing and they wanted a more immediate solution to their problem.

"I believe that anyone can make a difference. You don't have to be a straight-A student or a perfect person. You just have to know what you want and what is best. You have to be persistent."
—Ciara, High School Student

Many of the court cases mentioned in this chapter took much longer to resolve than the Bronx case because the cases involved a long legal procedure. Often, students are already out of school before the case is resolved. Despite the length of time it took to resolve their issues, students involved in the cases we've cited believed that their investment of time and effort was worth it because they paved the way for the students who came after them. If you have time to follow through on the process that a legal protest requires and if you believe your issue will have an impact on future classes, you may choose to proceed slowly and deliberately. Refer to chapter 2 for the different ways to lodge your protest.

MORE RESOURCES FOR HELP

There are many agencies, both local and national, that are dedicated to upholding teenagers' rights. Your school might have a list of agencies available in your city or town. For issues involving your constitutional rights, you can get information from your local ACLU. The national office is located at 125 Broad Street, 18th Floor, New York, NY 10004. You can find local offices through its website at www.aclu.org. If you are in college, check to see if the school has a local ACLU advocacy center.

Many law schools have interns to work on individual cases as part of their course work. Check with the law schools in your area to see if there are students available to work with you. Professors supervise these students, for example, in a law clinic. Be aware that if you choose this route, you are working with a student, who may have more time and energy to devote to your case but has limited experience. (See chapter 9 for more information about finding affordable or free legal representation.)

6 Learning Disabilities

Learning disabilities are unlike other disabilities because they can be well hidden. They are often referred to as the "invisible disability." A learning disability cannot be seen in the same way you see a physical disability. A learning disability affects the way you take in information, process that information, store the information, and then retrieve the information from memory to use it when you speak, write, or move. No two learning disabilities are alike.

Your learning disability may affect many aspects of your life. If you have been diagnosed with a learning disability, you might have difficulty with the activities of daily living, such as organization, learning, shopping, traveling, or making yourself understood. You know that you have more difficulty with tasks than most of the other students in your class or the other people who work with you.

A learning disability has been called a "problem," a "handicap," and a "learning difference." No matter what your learning disability is called, it means that it is a fact that you learn differently from the majority. However, you do learn! Your access to learning, work, and the other things that make up your life is just as important as it is for anyone without a learning disability. That access *can't* be denied.

The goal for any person, with or without a learning disability, is to lead a fulfilling life as independently as possible. It may be a little harder to accomplish this if you have a learning disability, and you might have to fight to get what you need. Self-advocacy is one of the most important skills for a student with a learning disability to acquire.

◎ **Self-advocacy means learning your rights.**

◎ **Self-advocacy means making sure you receive those rights.**

◎ **Self-advocacy helps you to make sure you are given the tools to reach your goals.**

Self-advocacy involves your rights in the legal sense, that is, rights that special education laws have determined you are entitled to. Self-advocacy also involves your ability to make decisions that affect your life in large and small ways, such as choosing your friends, deciding what to study in school, choosing what relationships to

**"Before I started [self-advocating], I was nervous about going up to teachers to ask for help. I was intimidated by them and embarrassed about my disability. Now I will talk to anyone about it."
—Jess, age fifteen**

have, and determining what type of job you want once you leave school. No one knows better than you do what you need. You also need to know how to get what you need.

In this chapter, we help you understand how to get what you need. We explain the laws that entitle you to a free and appropriate education (FAPE); we provide you with a step-by-step approach to being a successful advocate for yourself. We detail the steps to use when you believe that your school is not providing the appropriate services for you and it becomes necessary to file a complaint. We also list resources you can use to find additional help you might need in the defense of your rights.

WHAT'S HAPPENING TO YOU?

Because a learning disability is not always obvious to those around you, you can't expect others to know what you need unless you are able to tell them. While you are in school, special education teachers are mandated to make sure you get the instruction and accommodations you require based on their training and professional evaluations of your needs. Once you leave school, your needs will not be as clear to those around you. To be successfully independent, you must determine the accommodations you need to be successful in your workplace, in your living place, and in the world around you.

To get through school successfully, students with learning disabilities can benefit from the help of many adults. Teachers should meet with the parents of students with learning disabilities yearly, at the least, to talk about each student's specific learning disabilities and what the disabilities mean for the student, both academically and socially. Teachers, parents, and specialists in the field of educating students with learning diabilities must work to determine which classes students will be placed in and even to orchestrate appropriate, helpful, and fun after-school social activities.

Ideally, parents and teachers are, by training and interest, caregivers. Involved parents and teachers want the best for children and students and want to protect young people from hurt and failure. When parents and teachers educate themselves about their children's and students' needs, they can become skilled at helping children get the resources they need to be successful. If you are a student with a learning disability, you may have benefited from this type of care and concern. It can be a huge relief for a child not to have to make critical decisions about classes, activities, and

"Before it was easier when teachers did everything. When I advocate for myself I feel proud that I can do it."—Emily, age fifteen

friends. However, not all circumstances are ideal. If you believe the adults in your life have not done their best to identify and address your needs, educating yourself about the law can improve your situation. Even in exemplary circumstances, you must prepare for the time when adults will no longer take responsibility for you.

The federal law, the Individuals with Disabilities Education Act (IDEA), says that at age sixteen—which may seem as young an age to you as it may seem to your parents—you need to begin to take over some of that responsibility. The law requires that you begin to have a say in what happens to you when you turn sixteen. That will mean a lot of extra responsibility:

- You will need to be involved in planning for your future.
- You will need to begin to speak up for yourself.
- You will need to start standing up for what you want in order to be successful and happy.
- You will need to begin the path toward being self-sufficient.
- You will need to begin to advocate for yourself.

Whether or not you believe you've received excellent help and representation with your educational needs, learning how to self-advocate as early as you are able gives you an advantage in achieving success in school and in your life outside of school.

"If you don't self-advocate you won't get the things you need to do well. I've always been embarrassed about being in special education and have been made fun of. Now I see it as an advantage because I get the help. I now see it is not me, it is just the way I learn and I can ask for what I need or explain why it's difficult to do what I can't do."—Ashley, age sixteen

WHAT DOES THIS MEAN TO YOU?

Vincent Verrassi, Metropolitan Campus Director of the Regional Center at Fairleigh Dickinson University in New

Ashley.

Jersey, says, "You can't advocate for yourself unless you know what you need and what is different about you. Once you know that, the rest is mechanical." If you are in high school or even middle school, there are many resources at your school to help you learn what you need to know about yourself. Your individualized educational program (IEP) has a summary of your strengths and areas of difficulty. Your psychological test reports go into greater detail about your particular learning style and what makes you unique. If you have a teacher or guidance counselor you particularly respect, you can talk with him or her about how you seem to learn best. If you are out of high school, you can use the tools at the end of this chapter to help identify your strengths and challenges so you can reach a better understanding of yourself. Then, as Verrassi says, it will be easier to discover what you need to be successful, and you will be better able to advocate for what you need.

Each person with a learning disability has a specific set of strengths and challenges. The types of accommodations and training that help you be successful may be totally inappropriate for someone else. All people with learning disabilities can benefit from specific accommodations and

Keep in mind that there is no standardized formula to provide you with the tools you need to succeed as a person with learning disabilities. All of the accommodations you need must be based on your specific learning disability.

training in school and in the workplace. There are steps you can follow to make sure you get what you need.

WHAT ARE YOUR RIGHTS?

If you are eligible for special education services, you have specific rights under IDEA. IDEA is the federal law that guarantees the right to a FAPE for all students in the United States with learning disabilities between the ages of three and twenty-two (or until you graduate from high school). IDEA also mandates that transition services must be provided to ensure that students have the skills they need beyond high school. It allows you to and expects that you will attend your IEP meetings beginning at age sixteen (the new version of the federal law has changed this from age fourteen to sixteen, but many states have decided to continue beginning this process at age fourteen). It gives you the right to be educated with other students who are not disabled to the maximum extent appropriate. The law was put into effect in 1975 and is updated often, most recently in 2004.

The foundation of IDEA is the IEP, which describes the specific programs and services that must be provided for students who are eligible for special education services under IDEA. The IEP must be reviewed on a regular basis to make sure it continues to meet the student's needs. When you graduate from high school or reach age twenty-two, your rights under this law come to an end.

IDEA has specific rules about discipline and suspension for students who have an IEP. Before discipline or suspensions can be implemented, a determination must be made about whether the rules violation was a direct result of the student's disability. The decision is made using a procedure called a "manifestation determination," which analyzes the behavior and determines whether or not it is a result of the student's disability. For example, a student with a language-processing problem gets into fights because he doesn't understand the words and social cues other students use. The student's rules violation is probably a result of his disability and because of that, he cannot be disciplined in the same way that students without a language-processing disability would be disciplined. Instead, the special education team will be required to design a behavior plan that includes strategies to help him interact more appropriately.

The newest changes in IDEA make it the responsibility of the parent (instead of the school) to show that the student's action was a direct result of his or her disability. If the team finds that a behavior is not a result of the disability, the student can be disciplined in the same way as a student with no learning disability. (See chapter 5 for information on discipline procedures for students with no learning disabilties.)

If you choose to go to a private school at your own (or your parents') expense, you are still eligible for services under IDEA. You have a right to the services listed in your IEP, but you may have to access the services at your local public school. Check with your local school department to find out their policy for students who go to private schools. The Rehabilitation Act of 1973 provides states with federal money to fund vocational services for people with disabilities. Section 504 of the act is a civil rights act that prohibits discrimination against people with disabilities in any program that receives state funds. Public schools, most private schools, and most colleges receive state funds, so they are bound by the mandates of Section 504. The

It's important to be aware that, to be protected by the law, you must be qualified to do the college program or the job you want. Your disability does not give you an entitlement to a job or college admission. To receive accommodations, you must disclose your disability and request specific accommodations.

law gives you the right to accommodations to help you meet your needs to receive an education or to be able to do a particular job.

The Americans with Disabilities Act (ADA) of 1990 prohibits discrimination against people with disabilities. ADA applies to all public schools, most private schools, and colleges regardless of funding. It also applies to state and local governments and private employers with more than fifteen employees and to public services, transportation, public accommodations, and telecommunications.

To be considered to be eligible for accommodations under Section 504 and ADA, your disability must substantially limit a major life function. Because education and learning are major life activities, most people with learning disabilities are protected by these acts while in school. You must also have documentation of your disability to be regarded as having one.

The current Elementary and Secondary Education Act is known as No Child Left Behind (NCLB). The original act was passed in 1965, and it holds schools accountable for the progress of all students, including those with disabilities. It requires schools to measure and then report on the progress, or lack thereof, of all students to see whether the students are making improvements. The report that your school district prepares will give you and your family information about how well students with learning disabilities are educated in your local school system. NCLB also establishes guidelines for the accommodations students need to participate in assessments and for the qualifications of teachers who work with the students who have learning disabilities.

WHO HAS THE POWER TO HELP?

According to Daphne Gregory's Self-Advocacy Speakers' Bureau in Millburn, New Jersey, the most important person to help you achieve your goals is you. Ms. Gregory's students have

"Before being in self advocacy group, I was teased a lot. When I got called stupid and stuff, it made me feel I was stupid. My high school self-advocacy group taught me not be ashamed and embarrassed. Now if someone says something, I don't care."
—Jonathan, age fifteen

learned that if you can understand your disability and the accommodations you need to succeed, you will feel better about yourself and be able to advocate for yourself with your teachers.

Ms. Gregory's students learn to negotiate instead of reacting to teachers and getting into trouble in school. With the knowledge of self-advocacy they have acquired, the students hold an annual conference at their high school for students in other towns to teach them the advocacy skills they have learned. The students, along with their advisor, Ms. Gregory, have come up with positive steps that help students with learning disabilities work toward greater independence.

Ms. Gregory's students teach these steps toward self-advocacy:

The self-advocacy group at Milburn High School. Photo by Cheryl Tuttle.

Learn about Your Disability and Be Able to Define and Explain It to Yourself and Others

Use the Successful Self-Advocate Checklist in this chapter to help you focus on your strengths and challenges. Write out your answers and read them aloud until you feel confident talking with others about yourself.

Identify What Is Interfering with Your Success in or outside of School

If your teachers spend most of the time at the front of the class giving you information that you need to write down, you need to keep that information in mind while you are writing quickly, taking notes. Ask yourself: Can you do that?

SUCCESSFUL SELF-ADVOCATE CHECKLIST

Here is a successful self-advocate checklist developed by the Millburn High School Student Self-Advocacy Conference held in Millburn, New Jersey:

- What is a learning disability?
- What type of learning disability do I have?
- When learning new and difficult information through the visual, auditory, and haptic (touch/movement channel) what are my:
  - Strengths?
  - Challenges?
- How do I prefer to get information when learning difficult or unfamiliar information: visual, auditory, or haptic (touch/movement)?
- Describe how the following specific areas are directly affected by my learning disability and what are the compensations and accommodations I use:
  - Reading
  - Mathematics
  - Language
  - Spelling
  - Memory
  - Test taking
  - Concentration and attention
  - Impulsiveness
  - Organization and time management
  - Social perceptions and interactions
- In what ways does my learning disability have the potential to interfere with my job performance?
- What compensations or accommodations do I now use to improve my job performance?
- What is my role in the IEP process?
- What law protects me:
  - In high school?
  - In a post-secondary institution?
  - On the job?
- Name two famous people who have learning disabilities.
- I have another disability in the area of:

_____

_____

_____

⑨ **If your teachers expect you to get the subject matter by reading textbooks at home, you need to be able to read the grade-level texts easily.**

⑨ **Think about your teachers' teaching styles and try to see if they teach to the way that you learn.**

Learn How to Participate in Your IEP Meeting

An IEP meeting can be pretty intimidating. There are usually three or more adults there, including your teachers or administrators at your school, and they will all be talking about you. It is not easy to break into a group like that and speak assertively about what you think and what you need. Don't try to do everything at once. It is okay to be an observer at a few IEP meetings before trying to participate in one. Here are some tips to help you get ready to advocate for yourself at an IEP meeting:

⑨ **Become familiar with your IEP and look at it critically.**

⑨ **See what parts of it you agree with and which parts you disagree with.**

⑨ **Make notes on your copy so you can talk specifically about your concerns.**

⑨ **Watch and take notes on how the meeting progresses and pay attention to what each participant says and does.**

⑨ **Ask questions about anything you don't understand.**

⑨ **Write down what types of accommodations work for you and what your long-term goals are.**

⑨ **Practice saying what you think out loud so that it will seem more natural in the actual meeting.**

Having a learning disability means that it is more difficult for you to acquire and master information in the same way the majority of the other students in your school do. However, accommodations that you need in the classroom can help those other students as well. If you think of your disability as a problem or a handicap, you will have a harder time advocating for what you need to succeed.

ACCOMMODATIONS YOU HAVE
THE RIGHT TO REQUEST

Possible accommodations in high school:

- Allow for response to be verbal or dictated to a scribe or tape recorder,
- Permit assignments and notes via computer,
- Extended time for tests,
- Frequent breaks during tests,
- Tests given in a separate setting,
- Special test preparation,
- Preferential seating, or
- Directions read aloud.

Possible accommodations in college:

- Taped textbooks,
- Use of a tape recorder,
- Instructions given orally and in writing,
- A note taker,
- Priority seating,
- Extended time on tests or for assignments,
- Directions read aloud on tests, or
- A quiet room for tests.

Possible accommodations in your job:

- Instructions orally and in writing,
- Frequent and specific feedback about performance,
- Training courses,
- Frequent breaks, or
- Quiet workspace.

Explore Options and Accommodations
Available to You in and out of School

Look at the list of possible accommodations in this chapter. See if those or others that you think of would make a difference in your success. Talk with your teacher or employer to see if you can try them out. The technology available today has made a big difference in the possible accommodations available to students with learning disabilities. Go to an electronics store and look at the available computer software that would make it easier for you to take notes, do research, or complete your job. Don't be afraid to ask for an accommodation if you think it would work.

Develop a Backup Plan If Your Accommodation Requests Are Denied

Not all things are possible in a particular school or a job situation. It is a good idea to have a list of alternatives if what you want is not available. If the school will not allow laptop computers to be used in the classroom, see if you can have another student take notes for you. If the employer doesn't have a training program, see if there is someone there who can be a mentor for you until you learn how to do the job alone. If you cannot reach an agreement, use the negotiating skills discussed in chapter 2.

Practice Asking for What You Need in a Nonconfrontational Way

Chapter 2 has specific guidelines about how to present your case. You need to depersonalize and to know how and when to deliver your message. Review those guidelines before asking for what you need.

Evaluate How Your Efforts Worked and Revise and Rework as Necessary

It is rare that anyone gets 100 percent of what he or she wants the first time they ask. If you get what you want the first time, great. If not, you may need to go back to your team more than once to get what you need. Take stock of what you did to make your request and how you did it. Think about what worked and try to evaluate why that particular strategy worked. See if you can apply that strategy to your next goal. You might even ask the teacher or employer why your strategy didn't work and what he or she would suggest that you do the next time.

TRANSITION PLANNING

Students at Millburn High School in New Jersey, and other students who are successful self-advocates, did not get to that point by themselves. By participating in the Millburn High School Transition Program for four years, teens learned about the different types of learning disabilities, the way the brain works, different learning styles, the IEP process, and the specific laws and rights that are related to learning disabilities. They thought about their future plans and made sure they got the education and training they needed to accomplish their goals. They had encouraging parents, teachers, guidance counselors, and administrators who nurtured and taught and supported them.

Another student who has been successful in advocating for himself is Ari Ne'eman, a high school senior in 2006 and a person with Asperger's Syndrome. (Asperger's Syndrome is a type of autism that professionals consider a nonverbal learning disability. It is generally characterized by a unique means of social interaction and perception, as well as over-focusing in certain areas.) He spent time in a variety of full- and part-time special education placements, until he successfully advocated to be included in mainstream courses. He is now a frequent speaker on special education and Asperger's Syndrome for the New Jersey Department of Education and others.

According to Ari, "Transition is the most important issue in special education. Too many students 'in the system' are never really prepared for life after high school, because the school believes that they won't be able to succeed like more 'normal' kids can." To prepare for transition out of high school, Ari says, "Students need the opportunity to gain experience accomplishing their goals, on their own, while they are in high school. In college and the real world, the level of support for persons with learning differences is significantly less. Without the experience in facing their own challenges through self-advocacy, students often stagnate after high school."

Ari believes that an educational system that tells students that they have no power and that they are inferior to others is

Ari Ne'eman.

one of the biggest obstacles in learning to advocate for oneself. He believes the first step in the transition process is for students to "eliminate the fallacy of inferiority and be proud of your own abilities." He notes that because one type of life path (often chosen by the educational system) may be easier to accomplish as a result of the accommodations a student needs, students are often set on a path that doesn't relate to their interests. In Ari's view, "students will succeed when they feel a real passion for what they're doing, and they need to be able to advocate for themselves to make sure they can follow a path that makes sense for them."

Eliminating your feelings of inferiority and advocating for your interests and needs is not easy; even a successful self-advocate like Ari has had to develop the right strategies to achieve his goals. Ari says, "It's important to have resources that you can use and people who will work with you in getting what you want for your life. Sometimes the regular channels don't work for that, in which case advocating for yourself often means looking for more unconventional routes."

Identify the adults in your life who can help you get what you need to go where you want to go in life. Reach out to your teachers or to other adults in your community and talk with them about your needs and your goals. Find an adult you can work with over the long term. Find someone who treats you as an equal—a person who will focus on what you say and not just on your circumstances, history, or diagnosis. Listen to what they have to offer. When you do this, it is important to weigh the advice you are given to make sure it works for you. As stated in chapter 4, not all advice is good advice. Use the

Ari Ne'eman learned that there is more than one way to accomplish a goal. Ari wanted to take a college-level history course at his high school, both because he is interested in history and because he wanted the course to be listed on his transcript when he applied for college. "I had attempted to get access to the course repeatedly, but I was turned down because I was classified as a special ed student, despite the fact that I fulfilled the regular admission requirements. I decided I needed to pursue a different route. The class was an AP course, so the end goal was to get college credit by passing the final test. I studied on my own for the test, took the test, and passed with a five, the highest score possible for AP tests. I was given credit for the course (even though I didn't sit in on classes) and was able to take more APs the next year."

In 2006, Ari Ne'eman started to attend the University of Maryland–Baltimore County on a full academic scholarship as part of the Sondheim Public Affairs Scholars Program. He intended to pursue a career in law or economics. He also was appointed by New Jersey Governor Jon Corzine in 2006 to serve on the Special Education Review Commission for the State of New Jersey.

questions in that chapter to decide whether to accept the advice or not.

WHERE AND HOW TO START

Beginning at age fourteen or sixteen (depending upon the law in your state), there must be a "Statement of Transition Services Needs" in your IEP. This is a plan for what you need to successfully transition to the next step after high school. The plan is a long-range plan for your life beyond school. It can include specific instruction, employment opportunities, community experiences, independent living experiences, or functional vocational assessments to determine your specific

The federal law says that most transition services must start at sixteen. Many states begin this process earlier. If your state is one that uses sixteen as the starting age, you can request that the process begin earlier.

post–high school skills and interests. If you are planning to go to college, you need to make sure that you are taking the courses you need to get into a college of your choice. If you are planning to go into a job right after school, the plan needs to ensure that you get the skills you need to do that job. It is important that you take part in writing this plan so that it will reflect what you think you need to be successful after high school. In fact, the law says that your needs, skills, and hopes must be the foundation of that plan.

YOU MUST BE INVOLVED IN PLANNING YOUR FUTURE

The National Center for Learning Disabilities lists these additional steps for being your own advocate in high school:

- Attend all your IEP meetings and make sure that the specific accommodations that you need are listed in the plan.
- Set goals for yourself that are realistic. Get as much detail as possible about the various choices available to you.
- Be aware of what you are good at and what is a challenge for you. Think about what you enjoy doing and what you do well.
- Request that your school update your IEP before you leave the school so the IEP will have the most current information about you.

The National Center for Learning Disabilities has these suggestions if you are in college:

◎ Make sure you can document your disability when you arrive at college.

◎ Make sure you know your rights to participation in programs and activities at college and the accommodations that you can access there.

> "I think that [self-advocacy] is more like a choice. By [self-advocating] you make a choice about your future. You can sit there and not say anything or you can speak up. I make the choice every day by coming to school and getting the help I need. Someone is not going to do it for you in your life. You need to take control."—Brad, age seventeen

◎ Meet with your advisors to talk about your interests and challenges and any specific support you need.

WHERE ELSE TO GO

If you believe that you are being denied your rights under any of the laws listed previously, there are things you can do. Under IDEA, there are steps you need to take if you believe that you are not receiving a FAPE:

1. An official complaint to your local school system and the state education agency about what you believe is a violation of your IEP or services.

     ◎ The complaint must state the nature of the problem, any relevant facts relating to it, and a proposed resolution to the problem.

     ◎ Your local school administration department must respond to this type of complaint within ten days of receiving it. They

You and your family might want to get some help drafting your complaint so you don't lose valuable time. Call the parent advocacy organization in your state to see if it has samples of complaint letters. Your school should be able to provide you with the name of your local agency. You can also contact the National Center for Learning Disabilities at their address in this chapter.

must explain why they did or did not take a specific action, describe other options, and provide the basis for their recommendation.

◎ The school district must also notify the hearing officer at the state education agency. The hearing officer determines if the complaint can go forward.

◎ If the hearing officer thinks that the complaint is not specific enough, you have an opportunity to refile the complaint to make sure it can go forward. If this happens, the time line starts over and the school has an additional ten days to respond.

2. If the complaint goes forward, the school and your family may try to resolve the dispute through mediation or a resolution session.

◎ A resolution session, new to the law in the 2004 reauthorization, is an opportunity for you to meet with the people in your school system to discuss your complaint and to try to resolve the problem at the local level. If you reach an agreement at this level, you and the school sign a legally binding agreement. There are usually no lawyers at this type of session, unless you bring an attorney and the school brings one in response.

◎ Mediation is a procedure designed to bring about a peaceful settlement or compromise about your situation through an objective neutral party. Mediation offers an opportunity to discuss the problem with an independent person and provides an attempt to try to resolve the situation without hostility or legal action. If the complaint is resolved at this level, a legally binding agreement is also drawn up. Again, at this level, there are usually no lawyers present, so the process is less expensive and less adversarial. You do not have to pay for the mediator, the school does.

3. You also have the right to ask for an impartial hearing, either after you have tried mediation or a resolution hearing, or instead of either.

◎ An impartial hearing officer who is not employed by your state or local education agency usually conducts an impartial hearing. This officer must be objective and have no personal or professional interest that might conflict with that objectivity. The officer is often a lawyer who is hired for the purpose of the hearings who understands federal and state special education regulations, is able to conduct hearings, and can give an opinion based on the federal and state laws that govern special education in your state. (States have different guidelines for this procedure, so check the laws in your state.)

◎ The impartial hearing is also a means for resolving a complaint, but it is a more formal procedure and has many more rules and regulations. In many cases, parents bring an attorney who is familiar with disabilities law to an impartial hearing because it is a legal process and because the school district might have its own attorney there. The procedure is more costly because of the legal expenses, the time involved in getting materials together, talking with witnesses, and the many other aspects that are involved when you go to court. In some circumstances, if you win the case, the school district must pay the cost of your lawyer.

4. If the issue is not resolved at this level, you can challenge the decision of the impartial hearing in court. The school district can also challenge the decision if the district disputes it. At this point, the case can go to the U.S. district court or to another jurisdiction. Your lawyer will be involved at this point and will guide you through the process.

Your expenses are not automatically covered. If your district settles your claim before a final determination or you only receive part of what you ask for, the state may not be obligated to pay. Be sure you know all the facts before you take this step.

With Section 504, mediation is also a good first step for resolving disputes and would work similarly to mediation under IDEA. If your case falls under Section 504, and the complaint is against a school, you can contact the Office of Civil Rights at:

Office for Civil Rights
U.S. Department of Education
400 Maryland Avenue, S.W.
Washington, D.C. 20202-1100
1-800-421-3481
Fax: (202) 245-6840; TDD: (877) 521-2172
E-mail: OCR@ed.gov
www.ed.gov/ocr

If you believe your rights under ADA have been violated, you can call the ADA Information Line at 800-514-0301 for information about procedure. If you believe that you have been discriminated against in employment, you must file a complaint with the Equal Employment Opportunity Commission (EEOC) within eighteen days of the event. Every district has its own office, and you need to file through the office in your area. Check your phone book or look them up online at www.eeoc.gov/offices.html. You will need specific information to file the claim, and the EEOC can tell you what you need. Its national address is:

U.S. Equal Employment Opportunity Commission
1801 L Street, N.W.
Washington, D.C. 20507
Phone: (202) 663-4900
TTY: (202) 663-4494

If you believe you have been discriminated against by a state or local government agency or by a public accommodation, you can file a complaint with U.S. Department of Justice for investigation or go directly to federal court and file a lawsuit.

Under National Center for Learning Disabilities guidelines, if a school does not meet its academic goals for two consecutive years, you have the right to attend a nonfailing school, and the district must pay for your transportation to that school. You also may have the right to compensatory services, such as tutoring, after-school programs, and summer school, to be paid for by your district. NCLB is overseen at the state level, and states demand that school systems submit annual progress reports and methods for improving progress for all students.

MORE RESOURCES FOR HELP

If you think a transition program might be helpful in your high school, talk with your teachers and administrators to see if you can develop a program in your community. You can contact Ms. Daphne Gregory, Transition Specialist, at daphneg@optonline .net or (973)479-0272. There are many organizations and agencies at both the local and national levels that work with families and teens with learning disabilities. Check your local phone book or the Internet for organizations in your area. Some of the agencies at the national level are:

National Center for Learning Disabilities
381 Park Avenue South
Suite 1401

New York, NY 10016-8806
888-575-7373/212-545-7510
www.ncld.org

Children and Adults with Attention Deficit/
Hyperactivity Disorder
8181 Professional Place, Suite 150,
Landover, MD 20785
800-233-4050
www.chadd.org

International Dyslexia Association
8600 LaSalle Road, Chester Building #382
Baltimore, MD 21286-2044
410-296-0232
www.interdys.org

Learning Disabilities Association of America
4156 Library Road
Pittsburgh, PA 15234-1349
Phone (412) 341-1515 Fax (412) 344-0224
www.ldaamerica.org

Learning Disabilities Worldwide, Inc.
PO Box 142 Weston, MA 02493
781-890-5399
www.ldworldwide.org

7 Physical Disabilities

Physical disabilities come in all shapes and sizes: You may have impaired vision or hearing, weakness or paralysis in your limbs, an inability to walk, to speak, or even to move voluntarily. Your physical disability may be obvious to all if you require a wheelchair or other device to help you move, or it might be invisible to most people until a barrier gets in your way. You have the right to enjoy the same opportunities as people without disabilities, but you may need to advocate for those rights, either as part of a group or on your own.

Rajiv.

"I was born in Calcutta, India, and there were no proper treatments for pregnant women so that means that many babies were born with birth defects. I was born deaf with cerebral palsy, the one that caused me to be quadriplegic at birth. Communications are very difficult, especially phone calls, because many people do not understand how to use relay services. Due to my deafness, people need to communicate by speaking slowly and writing on a paper. I type using my big toe on my left foot. I can do finger spelling, and using the communications device to communicate with others.

"I am satisfied with my disabilities, even though I get frustrated sometimes and people need to stop being afraid of people with disabilities. I may be deaf and quadriplegic, but I am just a typical guy who enjoys helping others and I am capable of doing various kinds of things. I believe that it is very important for people to have an equal opportunity to live, learn, socialize, and work, no matter how people look at the disabled.

"Beyond college, I would like to relocate and open my own business to help people with disabilities to follow their dreams and help them focus on what they CAN do. I am currently serving on the Kids as Self Advocates [KASA] advisory board. I am involved with KASA, because I believe that it is very important to work together to educate the community about disability issues. People should be more aware of people with disabilities and teach the 'able-bodied' world that we are just like them, 'just a little broken.'"—Rajiv, college student

In this chapter, we discuss the federal laws that define the rights and accommodations that are available to teens with physical disabilities in school, the workplace, and daily life. Knowing the law will give you a better understanding of what your rights are. With knowledge about the history and about issues that concern you and with information about possible accommodations in the many areas of your life, you will be a better advocate for needed changes. We also provide you with resources where you can get additional information about your rights and show you how to use your self-advocacy skills to improve the quality of your life based on your personal needs and wants.

WHAT'S HAPPENING TO YOU?

Barriers that interfere with your ability to participate fully in school, in the workforce, and in the basic activities of daily living are complex and varied. There is no singular solution to the many obstacles that get in the way of individuals with physical disabilities, but the obstacles are there and they get in *your* way. For example:

- **If you have impaired vision: When you are in school, are you assigned a seat that allows you a close and clear line of sight to the teacher and the blackboard or are you assigned a classroom seat alphabetically?**

- **If you have impaired mobility that may not be visibly obvious: Does your school or after-school workplace have ramps, elevators, and accessible doorknobs and bathrooms or are you forced to accommodate yourself to an inaccessible environment?**

- **Do you believe there are there activities that take place during your school day, in your social activities, in your workplace, at your church, or in your local movie theater that are denied to you because of your disability?**

- **Does your inability to hear make it difficult or impossible for you to take lecture-based courses in school or to communicate with your doctor or with other medical professionals?**

- **Do the physical barriers in your workplace prevent you from performing your job effectively or even keep you from holding the job?**

- **Do physical barriers of any sort prevent you from participating fully in your life?**

What would make your life easier? Think about what you want to do that you would be better able to do with an accommodation. Think about how that accommodation could be put into place.

WHAT ARE YOUR RIGHTS?

There are two laws that guarantee your rights if you have a disability: the Americans with Disabilities Act (ADA), Public

"I was diagnosed with diabetes in 4th grade and every year since then I have made it a habit to approach my teachers at the beginning of each school year and inform them of my condition. I have found that being open and honest with my teachers about managing my diabetes allows me to feel comfortable about doing things such as checking my blood sugar or giving myself a shot of insulin right in class. I make sure to tell my teachers that sometimes I might have a low blood sugar and I will need to just quietly slip out of class and go to the nurse's office. Being up front about what I need is an effective method because my teachers appreciate being in the know and are therefore understanding when I may have to leave class.

"I am also up front with my classmates about my diabetes and try to answer any questions they may have. Most of them are understanding, and I have only had one encounter where I had to stand up for myself against a classmate's teasing. I was in 6th grade and a boy in my class saw me eating a snack and started making fun of me. I told him calmly but firmly that I was having a low blood sugar and eating a snack was a necessity. After I explained the situation to him, he understood and apologized. My honesty with people about what I may need to do sometimes as a diabetic has served me well."—Meaghan, age seventeen

Law 101-336, passed in 1990; and Section 504 of the 1973 Rehabilitation Act. These acts make it illegal to discriminate on the basis of disability in employment, in services provided by state and local governments, and in schools, public places, transportation, and use of telecommunications services. For the purpose of these acts, a person with a disability is defined by the ADA as "a person who has a physical or mental impairment that substantially limits one or more major life activities, a person who has a history or record of such an impairment, or a person who is perceived by others as having such an impairment." The ADA is a civil rights law. Under ADA, it is illegal for an employer to discriminate against you in hiring,

Meaghan.

firing, promotion, and retention simply because of a disability, if you can perform the job either with or without accommodations.

Having a disability will not *get* you a job, and it will not allow you to keep a job if your disability makes that job impossible for you to do. However, if you are qualified to do the job, but need special accommodations, such as adaptive equipment, a modified work schedule, or special supports, the employer must provide for and pay for these accommodations, if it is not too expensive or too difficult to accomplish.

Keep in mind that the law applies to companies that have twenty-five or more employees.

If you work while you are in high school, you will get an idea of what types of accommodations you will need in your workplace once you are out of school. With that knowledge, you will have a better idea about what work you will be able to do and what aids you will need before beginning your job search. When you apply for a job, you will need to be specific about your disability and about the adaptations that will allow you to perform a particular job. Your employer gets to choose the reasonable accommodation to offer you, so have a few choices and a backup plan when you go. The employer does not have to provide an accommodation if it causes an undue hardship or compromises safety.

According to the ADA, "Reasonable accommodations remove obstacles to employment that prevent persons with disabilities from applying for and performing jobs. These barriers may be physical impediments, such as inaccessible facilities or equipment, or inflexible rules, such as when or how a job is performed." Call the ADA information line at 800-514-0301 (voice)/800-514-0383 (TDD) or your local field office of U. S. Equal Employment Opportunity Commission (EEOC) for more information. You can find your local field office on the EEOC website at www.eeoc.gov or by calling 800-669-4000.

ADA also requires that state and local government offices and programs be accessible to people with disabilities, including access to services, to programs, and to buildings that are run by your community or your state. City buses must have wheelchair lifts and voice information for blind travelers. City buildings must have ramps or elevators, and the elevators must have accommodations for the blind or partially sighted. 911 emergency equipment must have a Telecommunications Device for the Deaf (TDD) for people who are hearing impaired or speech impaired. If your community runs recreation programs, you must be able to get to them and be able to participate in them.

Title III of the ADA requires that public accommodations provide their services to people with disabilities in the most integrated way possible. Public businesses, such as restaurants, theaters, doctor's offices, and retail shops, must also be accessible to you. You need to be able to get into and out of the establishments and to be safe while you are there. Public accommodations can include ramps for wheelchairs and accessible bathrooms. Even shopping centers and the stores in them must be accessible. You have a right to shop throughout all areas of stores and to be able to view the items that are available for sale in an unimpeded way.

Many of the regulations of ADA are national issues, and many accommodations have already been made. Major cities and many small communities have built curb cuts into sidewalks that enable people in wheelchairs to maneuver from the sidewalk to the street. New school buildings with more than one floor must have elevators, and many older school buildings are having elevators installed. In buildings both large and small, number plates in elevators have raised Braille numerals, as well as recorded voices that call out floor numbers as they are passed. ADA also covers the use of service dogs to aid persons with seeing, hearing, balance, and psychiatric disabilities. ADA even covers the use of animals who are trained to alert their owners to an oncoming epilepsy seizure. A good deal of progress has been made in complying with the provisions of ADA, but there is still room for improvement.

At this writing, Section 504, also a civil rights law, is not as widely understood as ADA. Section 504 prohibits discrimination in public and private programs and in activities that receive federal funding. The law includes public high schools and colleges that receive any federal funds—and most do. Institutions that receive federal funds are required to provide reasonable accommodations and aids that students might need to access, participate in, and benefit from the educational

Don't hesitate to advocate for what you need! Remember that providing an accommodation for you does not mean that others will be shortchanged.

109

programs and other activities offered to all students. School systems are just starting to understand how Section 504 applies to students with disabilities. Often when a student needs an accommodation, the accommodation is a first-time occurrence for that school system. Educators may need to be educated about why an accommodation is *essential* for a student's full participation. That's where self-advocacy comes in.

WHAT DOES THIS MEAN TO YOU?

There any many types of barriers. As a result of advanced technology, there are many more accommodations available today. Each barrier and accommodation is specific to your situation. It is not possible to list them all in a book of this scope. A few examples include the following:

- ◉ **You are a great sprinter but can't go to school track meets because there is no place for you to change your insulin catheter.**
- ◉ **Your arthritis makes it difficult for you to take notes in class, but you could pass the course if you were able to get the notes another way.**
- ◉ **Your hearing impairment makes it impossible for you to benefit from lectures without a sign-language interpreter.**
- ◉ **Your attention deficit disorder keeps you from completing a test that you can pass but not in the same time limits as other students.**
- ◉ **Your wheelchair makes it impossible for you to get into the local movie theater where you want to go with your friends.**

There are reasonable accommodations that can be provided to address the issues listed here and many other issues. Accommodations can give you the same opportunities as the other students in your school, your friends after school, or other employees at your job. Many types of accommodation might be appropriate for you.

Not all accommodations are covered by ADA and Section 504. At times, you will have personal goals that are specific to

"When I ask people for help sometimes I get a little nervous. It is not always easy to ask for help. I often have to think about how to ask the questions. When I finally ask for help—with doors and reaching for things that are too high—I am relieved that I finally did it."—Julia, a fourteen-year-old student with spina bifida who must use a wheelchair

you and your situation. When that type of situation occurs, you will need to raise the awareness of the people around you about what you are capable of and about what you need to participate to the fullest extent you possibly can. Teens with physical disabilities have a range of abilities and needs, and they are as individual as you are. For a majority of people with disabilities, prejudice is a far greater problem than their impairment. If you want to live independently, you will need to overcome society's predetermined ideas about how and where people with your type of disability should live.

Julia. Photo by Cheryl Tuttle.

You have a right to equality and inclusion! Advocate to make your life the best it can be. The steps outlined in chapter 2 are not designed just for obtaining your legal rights. Self-advocacy is a lifelong process. The strategies you learn in this book can be used on a daily basis to negotiate all aspects of your life.

WHERE AND HOW TO START

If you believe that you are being denied access to educational, recreational, or employment opportunities because of your physical disability, start your self-advocacy process by talking with your parents, school advisors, or doctors. Even though you plan to do the advocacy yourself, it is a good idea to brainstorm the problems and discuss possible solutions with others who know your situation.

Once you are clear about the problem you want to resolve and possible solutions to the problem, the first step is to come up with a safe, reasonable way to talk directly with your teachers, employers, building owners, or community officials—whoever can directly affect a solution. It's possible that the people responsible for the barriers you encounter never thought about the issues you face every day and that lack of awareness is the only reason they never considered the accommodations you need. The people in charge just may need to have their sensitivity raised to accommodate your needs. They might even come up with better ideas than those you've thought of. Speaking up may be the only action you needed to take to find a solution!

However, it's wise to plan on encountering resistance and prepare to go further. Some establishments you encounter might be in compliance with the letter of the law but not its spirit. For example, a restaurant might consider itself wheelchair accessible if people are available to lift you and your wheelchair over the steps at the entrance. Even though it is legal, a remedy like that does not allow you to be independent and is an insult to your dignity.

WHO HAS THE DECISION-MAKING AUTHORITY?

If after taking that first approach, you do not believe that your issue is being solved, you may need to go to the next level. Follow the steps outlined in chapter 2 on how to be your own advocate. Ask your teacher, principal, or employer what organization or person is in charge of issues such as yours, and ask for specific contact information. When you find out who has the decision-making authority in your situation, write a letter to or make an appointment to talk with that person. In some cases, you might need to go even further. Even if you don't make progress on your first or second effort, don't give up if you feel you have a legitimate case. Look carefully at your facts and talk to the important adults in your life to help you confirm that your cause is just and that the barriers you face are morally, ethically, or legally wrong. Determine if the rights you are guaranteed by the laws in your case are being violated. If so, you can appeal to the agencies that oversee those laws. You may need to provide proof of your disability in writing to be covered by the ADA and Section 504.

If you believe your rights under ADA have been violated, you can call the ADA information line at 800-514-0301 for information about the procedures to follow when filing a complaint. If you believe that you have been discriminated against in employment, you will need to file a complaint with the EEOC within 180 days of the event. It must be filed by mail or in person at your local field office. (You can find your local field office on the EEOC website at www.eeoc.gov/ or by calling 800-669-4000.) You must have the following information:

- Your name, address, and telephone number;
- The name, address, and telephone number of the employer you believe has discriminated against you, and the number of employees in the business, if known;

◎ **A short description of the alleged event or discrimination that caused you to believe that your rights were violated; and**

◎ **The date(s) of the alleged violation(s).**

If the discrimination has been committed by a state or local government agency or by a public accommodation, you can file a complaint with the U. S. Department of Justice to request an investigation or file a lawsuit in federal court. If your case falls under Section 504, and the complaint is against a school, you can contact the U. S. Office of Civil Rights at:

Office for Civil Rights
U. S. Department of Education
400 Maryland Avenue, S.W.
Washington, D.C. 20202-1100
1-800-421-3481
Fax: (202) 245-6840; TDD: (877) 521-2172
E-mail: OCR@ed.gov
www.ed.gov/ocr

WHAT ARE ALTERNATIVE SOLUTIONS?

If you need ideas about possible aids that will help you overcome physical barriers, many organizations can help you figure out what is best for your specific issue. The Job Accommodation Network (JAN), 1-800-526-7234, is an agency that provides advice about individualized accommodations in the workplace. JAN might be a good place to get some ideas about what you need if you are not yet sure. JAN has consultants who specialize in specific disabilities, and you will be referred to the one that best suits your needs. This is a free service.

WHAT OTHER RESOURCES MIGHT PROVIDE HELP?

There are many agencies advocating for individuals with physical disabilities. A comprehensive, although not exhaustive, list is included here.

Access Now, Inc.
www.adaaccessnow.org/home.htm
19333 West Country Club Drive #1522
Aventura, Florida 33180
Tel. 305 705-0059 Fax 305-574-0341
Access Now is a Florida-based agency that is trying to spread
the word about possible accommodations so that agencies and
businesses will make the necessary alterations on their own
without having to be forced to by legal action or settlements.

American Association of People with Disabilities
www.aapd.com
AAPD National Headquarters
1629 K Street NW, Suite 503
Washington, DC 20006
202-457-0046 (V/TTY)
800-840-8844 (Toll Free V/TTY)
The AAPD helps students and job seekers with physical
disabilities by allowing them to watch a person at a
particular job to see what is involved and by career
exploration; the organization works with Congress to
promote laws and policies to help people with physical
disabilities lead independent lives.

The Center on Human Policy
Syracuse University
805 South Crouse Avenue
Syracuse, NY 13244-2280
Phone: (315) 443-3851 or 1-800-894-0826
Fax: (315) 443-4338
TTY: (315) 443-4355
www.thechp.syr.edu
The center is a Syracuse University–based policy, research,
and advocacy organization involved in the national
movement to ensure the rights of people with disabilities.
The center has been involved in the study and promotion of
open settings (inclusive community opportunities) for
people with disabilities.

Disability Rights Education and Defense Fund (DREDF)
2212 Sixth Street
Berkeley, CA 94710
510.644.2555 V/TTY
510.841.8645 fax
www.dredf.org
DREDF is a national center dedicated to protecting and
advocating for the civil rights of people with disabilities.

Kids as Self Advocates (KASA)
Julie Sipchen
KASA Project at Family Voices
2340 Alamo SE, Suite 102
Albuquerque, NM 87106
tel: 773-338-5541
fax: 773-338-5542
www.fvkasa.org
KASA helps health care professionals, policymakers, and
other adults in communities understand what it is like to live
with disabilities and helps teens learn how to advocate for
themselves.

8 Sexuality

As a young person, you are especially vulnerable to discrimination, harassment, and abuse as a result of your sexuality and your gender. Despite Title IX, the federal law that prohibits gender discrimination, and Title VII, the federal law that prohibits sexual harassment, both discrimination and harassment continue to confront many teens. Sexual harassment and gender discrimination are pervasive problems for teens in schools, in sports, in the workplace, and in many areas of everyday life. Sexual abuse, a crime with severe penalties, may occur in family, dating, or other relationships. Teens who are not provided with comprehensive sexuality education are not well equipped to understand their own bodies. Pregnancy, disease prevention, and self-protection from physical and emotional injury are more readily accomplished when you have the information you need!

It is frustrating and hurtful when you face discrimination for your gender, sexual identity, or sexual orientation. It is frightening and dangerous when adults or other teens make suggestive remarks to you or physically or emotionally pressure you to have sexual relations. It becomes criminal when adults or more powerful teens force you to have sex. In the worst cases, family members or other teens in dating relationships betray positions of power and trust by sexually and emotionally abusing young people in their care. As wonderful and powerful as the Internet can be, weblogs ("blogs") and "friendship" websites offer predators new opportunities to pretend to be teens to entice young people to meet them for sex.

It is unfair, unjust, and illegal for you to endure discrimination, harassment, or inappropriate sexual behavior or worse, outright abuse, from anyone, whether that person is an adult or another teen. In this chapter, we discuss your rights under Title VII and Title IX, what sexual harassment and gender discrimination are, and what to do to advocate for yourself if you are being harassed, discriminated against, or abused. We discuss fact-based, comprehensive, and responsible sexuality education, which can give you information to help you make judgments about your sexuality and what is happening to your body as it matures sexually. We discuss how to protect yourself from those who endanger you physically and sexually. We provide information on pregnancy prevention, disease prevention, and what your options are if you become pregnant. We offer a special section on teen dating violence.

WHAT ARE YOUR RIGHTS?

You have the right to fair treatment and sexual safety in school, at work, and at home, including on the Internet.

At School

Title IX of the Education Amendments of 1972 is enforced by the Office of Civil Rights. It is a federal statute prohibiting sex discrimination in education programs and activities that receive federal financial assistance. The increase in quality athletic programs for girls over the past several decades is directly connected to enforcement of Title IX (www.dol.gov/oasam/regs/statutes/titleix.htm).

Sexual harassment is prohibited in federally funded educational programs and activities under Title IX because sexual harassment is a form of discrimination. Conduct by an adult or another student in a school (verbally, nonverbally, or physically) is considered sexually harassing if it is severe, persistent, and pervasive and limits your ability to participate in education or school activities or creates a hostile environment in the school.

If your school has a policy against discrimination and harassment, the administrators of the school are showing that they are serious and concerned. Such a policy conveys the school's concern to the staff and student body. A school policy helps all students and staff in the school understand what sexual harassment is, clarifies the school's stand on discrimination and harassment, and tells everyone that violations will not be tolerated. A policy helps you know how to submit a grievance if you feel you have been harassed. Grievance policies must be stated in writing, posted in a place where they are accessible, and distributed to all students and parents, often in the school handbook usually provided at the start of the school year.

If your school does not have such a policy, it is in violation of Title IX and risks having government funding cut off. It is your right to request a copy of your school's policy against discrimination and harassment if you have never seen it. It is also your right to request that a policy be written if none exists. To advocate getting your school to write an antidiscrimination policy, follow the steps in chapter 2 and use the information in this chapter, including the Resources section. Your advocacy to get a policy written and implemented will benefit you and your fellow students.

At Work

Title VII of the Civil Rights Law of 1964 prohibits discrimination in the workplace. Title VII states: "it shall be an unlawful employment practice for an employer . . . to discriminate against any individual with respect to his compensation, terms, conditions, or privileges of employment, because of such individual's race, color, religion, sex, or national origin."

Many people were unclear about what types of behavior and what kind of employment atmosphere the law against harassment covered. The Supreme Court clarified what constitutes harassment when it issued several decisions in 1998. The first of those, *Oncale v. Sundowner Offshore Services, Inc.,* a unanimous decision in March 1998, stated: "When the workplace is permeated with discriminatory intimidation, ridicule, and insult that is sufficiently severe or pervasive to alter the conditions of the victim's employment and create an abusive working environment, Title VII is violated." Since that decision and others, most sexual harassment claims have been made under Title VII.

Also, the federal Equal Employment Opportunity Commission (EEOC) has defined sexual harassment as "unwelcome sexual advances, requests for sexual favors, and other verbal or physical conduct of a sexual nature . . . when . . . submission to or rejection of such conduct is used as the basis for employment decisions . . . or such conduct has the purpose or effect of . . . creating an intimidating, hostile or offensive working environment." The laws were written to protect you, not just adults. If you believe you are being sexually harassed, the person harassing you is breaking the law. Here are steps to follow, including reading the steps in chapter 2:

- ◎ Write down the type of behavior that you are experiencing. Be specific about the times and dates the harassment occurs, about who is doing the harassing, and about what the person or people are saying or doing to you. This is called "documentation." Documentation doesn't have to be fancy, but it should be as complete as possible, so you have a written history of what you're going through.

- ◎ If the harassment is occurring at your job, speak to your supervisor or your employer privately, following the guidelines in chapter 2. Bring your documentation notes with you. You want the adults you talk with about the harassment to believe what you say and to take action on your behalf. When you show them you have kept track of what's happened, they will know that you are serious about your complaint.

- ◎ If the harassment is occurring at school, review the school's harassment policy, and then speak to a trusted teacher or counselor at the school. Bring your documentation notes with you. Be prepared to discuss your issue with the school principal. Again, your documentation will show that you are serious.

For more information and guidance about how to deal with sexual harassment and discrimination, visit the American Civil Liberties Union (ACLU) Student Rights websites: www.aclu.org/standup/issues/and www.aclu.org/studentsrights/index.html.

◎ If you do not feel heard by your employer or school officials, you could file a grievance. Many businesses have procedures to follow when filing a grievance, so ask your supervisor to tell you what that procedure is and how to go about making a formal complaint. Your school's policy against discrimination and harassment should provide a grievance procedure to follow, so ask your guidance counselor or school principal for assistance.

◎ If you are still frustrated by adult reaction to your concerns, contact the children's law center in your state (these are often connected with law schools. See chapter 9 for details.) Children's law centers offer information and representation at low or no cost.

At Home and in Personal Relationships

Sexual abuse and sexual violence are serious crimes. If you feel threatened in a personal relationship or a friend is being threatened, whether it is by a boyfriend or girlfriend, a family member, or any adult, it is important that you act quickly to protect yourself or your friend. Speaking up is an important first step in self-advocacy against sexual abuse. Tell the person who is sexually threatening you to stop and to stop now! Tell the person that you know what he or she is doing is morally wrong and illegal.

Sexual abuse is more complicated and dangerous than other issues related to self-advocacy. One thing is the same: Know your audience, that is, try your best to figure out how dangerous the person abusing you might become. If the person pressuring or threatening you might hurt you, try hard to get away from that person immediately. Go to a safe place: a friend's home, your house of worship, your local hospital's emergency department, or the closest police station. Many communities have emergency abuse hotlines that are staffed 24 hours each day. Call 911! Your local police can pick you up if you feel unsafe and help you contact a hotline. If you call a hotline, the organization may be able to find you an emergency "safe home" right away.

Immediately tell a trusted adult or a mature, trusted friend what is happening to you, even if you don't think you are in immediate danger. Be aware that teachers, counselors, members of the clergy, and other adults who work with young people are "mandated reporters." That means that when they suspect or learn of abuse being perpetrated on a young person, they must report the information to the appropriate authorities, including your state's department of social welfare or social services and if necessary, the police.

> "I learned what a healthy and unhealthy relationship was, also how to prevent abuse from happening and many other important subjects."—Peer Leader from Help for Abused Women and their Children (HAWC) Lend UR Voice program, ninth grade

If you have been abused or raped, don't be ashamed; it is not your fault that an adult or a more powerful teen has hurt you. It is important that you seek medical help right away! Medical professions will immediately address the trauma of your abuse, help prevent pregnancy and STD infection, test for HIV infection, and arrange for counseling to help you cope with what has happened to you. If you aren't able to get immediate help from a family doctor, go yourself or have someone you trust or the police take you to your nearest emergency department. Doctors and nurses there will treat your injuries, test to see if you have been exposed to STDs, and if you are female, can take steps to be sure you don't become pregnant.

The hospital staff will be required to notify the police about the rape. Your confidentiality will be closely guarded, but the police will question you about the circumstances of the crime. There are rape crisis centers throughout the country to contact by phone for advice during this process. In many cases, a rape crisis counselor can accompany you during your physical examination and during questioning. Most domestic abuse and rape crisis organizations can assist you with obtaining a restraining order in court to prevent your abuser from contacting or even coming near you.

Rape is a serious crime. Many rapes go unreported because victims have been deeply traumatized by the attack on them, and they don't want to expose themselves to further trauma by pressing charges against the rapist. If you have been raped and feel unsure about pressing charges, consider that prosecuting the rapist would be the ultimate act of self-advocacy. The rapist's violence toward you should be prosecuted, both to give you justice and to prevent the rapist from harming others. A rape crisis counselor can help you talk this through and help you to make the decision that's right for you.

Online

With the rise of Internet use among teens, especially teen-oriented sites like MySpace.com and Facebook.com, young people are vulnerable to an aggressive group of adult predators. You may think that your friends—both in your real life and your online "friends list"—are the only people who will read your blogs or your MySpace information. Unless you always use the locks MySpace and other blog communities provide, that is not so. Everything you write in a blog or list as information on your MySpace page is public information, available to all, including your parents and people who may want to hurt you.

Self-advocacy always starts with information: Keep in mind that the Internet is the *World Wide Web*, so literally anyone in the world can read everything you write. Keep the personal information in your blogs and Web pages limited, especially contact information. If you start chatting online with someone who wants to meet you in person, back off! If someone you meet online sounds suspicious or too good to be true, he or she probably is. Immediately stop chatting with that person and inform an adult, including the local police, that someone may be trying to take advantage of you. The police may be able to intervene with the predator to catch and prosecute him or her. Please don't hesitate to seek help! Your health and well-being, now and in the future, are at stake!

SEXUAL ORIENTATION AND GENDER IDENTITY

Although adults and young people have become more open to teens' same-sex or other sexual orientations, there remain many individuals and groups who are opposed to any orientation other than heterosexual. If you identify yourself as gay, lesbian, bisexual, transgender, or questioning, you may fear discrimination. You may be afraid to tell your friends or adults of your sexual orientation because you can't predict the consequences. Will your friends abandon you? Will your parents ask you to leave their home? Will you be allowed to participate in school or work activities? Will you be denied admission to the college or job opportunity of your choice? Will you be the subject of harassment or discrimination? Constant concern about your orientation and gender identity can affect your emotional well-being as well as your school or job performance. If you don't have information about sexual orientation, you may have fears based on concerns for a friend. Or you may not understand about gender discrimination issues and the laws that may affect your behavior. Understanding the issues, and knowing your rights and the rights of your friends, is crucial to advocate for yourself, your friends, or your family.

There is no federal law that prohibits discrimination based on sexual orientation in private employment. However, there is an executive order outlawing discrimination based on sexual orientation in federal government. Many counties, cities, and states have laws that prohibit discrimination in private employment. (A list of states, cities, and counties that have laws prohibiting discrimination based on sexual orientation can be found at www.lambdalegal.org.) As with Title IX, other antidiscrimination laws affecting private employment, such as Title VII of the Civil Rights Act of 1964, have sections that deal with harassment and emotional distress that can be used to file a grievance about treatment that makes your workplace uncomfortable or affects your employment status based on your sexual orientation.

You may believe that you are being discriminated against at your school, whether through inappropriate touching, subtle slights by teachers or coaches, or by outright insults spoken by fellow students or school staff. Young people your age are usually fearful of people and things that are "different" and may not know how to react appropriately when they are around teens who identify as gay. It's not possible, however, to excuse discriminatory behavior on the part of adults, particularly adults who work with kids. If your school has an antidiscrimination policy, that may provide a method for filing a grievance against a teacher or other school staff member or against a harassing individual or group of students.

What You Can Do

Many young people have formed gay/straight alliances (GSAs) in their schools. GSAs are helpful both as a place to meet and as a way of educating schoolmates, teachers, administrators, and the community about sexual orientation. If you and your friends believe that a discriminatory atmosphere exists in your school, use the resources in this chapter to learn about starting a GSA. It may be necessary to get approval to create a GSA in your school, whether from the principal or the school board or both. Follow the steps in chapter 2 to educate and advocate for GSA approval. One organization, the Gay, Lesbian, and Straight Educational Network, www.glsen.org/cgi-bin/iowa/all/home.html, is dedicated to making sure that

Raymond Davidson felt discriminated against at his high school in New Jersey. With the help of GLSEN he was able to advocate for establishing a GSA at the school. His self-advocacy project took persistence, he says. "I would go in to the office to talk to the principal. If I was told that he was busy I would wait and miss as many classes as necessary to get my point across."

He advises young people who self-advocate to make sure they learn how to advocate properly. "You must follow the chain of command. Don't go right to the school board," he says, but rather start discussions with the school principal. "If the principal doesn't work, go to the superintendent. If the superintendent doesn't work, then go to the school board. Don't let the school board toss you around. Know your laws."

schools are safe for all students. GLSEN's mission states that the organization "strives to assure that each member of every school community is valued and respected regardless of sexual orientation or gender identity/expression."

Most important, know that you are not alone! Many resources, including sample antiharassment policies, are available from other organizations, including those listed at the end of this chapter. The ACLU's "Get Busy, Get Equal" website, www.aclu.org/getequal, is one such site. *Making Schools Safe* is an ACLU educational program about creating a workshop for faculty and students to address harassment based on gender identity in schools. ACLU affiliates in your state can provide you with more information about groups that are working to promote safer schools.

Raymond Davidson. Photo by Cheryl Tuttle.

PREGNANCY DISCRIMINATION

Title IX, which prohibits sex discrimination in the schools, is the law that covers pregnancy discrimination in school. If you are a teen who becomes pregnant while attending school, your pregnancy should not have an effect on your school status in any way. Any attempt to coerce or force you to leave school or attend an "alternative" school during or after your pregnancy is a clear violation of Title IX. You may not be barred from any school activity because of your pregnancy. If you attend a private school and are on scholarship, your school may not revoke your scholarship because of your pregnancy. If you are an athlete, you may not be removed from your athletic team because of your pregnancy, and when you return to school, you must be reinstated to the same status on your team that you had before your pregnancy.

Schools must treat your pregnancy as they would another student's temporary disability. So, if you become pregnant, you must be allowed to receive accommodations that allow you to continue to attend classes and keep up with your course work, to make up course work, and to take a leave of absence while

@@@@@@@@@@@@@@@@

**TITLE VII AMENDMENT PROHIBITING
PREGNANCY DISCRIMINATION**

The 1992 amendment to Title VII prohibiting pregnancy discrimination states:

If an employee is temporarily unable to perform her job due to pregnancy, the employer must treat her the same as any other temporarily disabled employee. For example, if the employer allows temporarily disabled employees to modify tasks, perform alternative assignments, or take disability leave or leave without pay, the employer also must allow an employee who is temporarily disabled due to pregnancy to do the same.

Pregnant employees must be permitted to work as long as they are able to perform their jobs. If an employee has been absent from work as a result of a pregnancy-related condition and recovers, her employer may not require her to remain on leave until the baby's birth. An employer also may not have a rule that prohibits an employee from returning to work for a predetermined length of time after childbirth.

Employers must hold open a job for a pregnancy-related absence the same length of time jobs are held open for employees on sick or disability leave.

you deliver the baby and recover from the delivery. Your leave must be granted for as long as your doctor believes you need to be away from school. Once you return to school, Title IX requires that you be reinstated to your courses and activities in the same way that a student who took a leave for temporary disability would be reinstated.

Title VII of the Civil Rights Act of 1964 was amended in 1992 to prohibit pregnancy discrimination in employment and is applicable to businesses that employ fifteen or more people. According to the law, employers may not discriminate against pregnant women in hiring or in employment practice.

Pregnancy and Disease Prevention, Abortion, and Abortion Alternatives

If you are a sexually active teen in either a homosexual or heterosexual relationship, it is your responsibility, whether you are a male or a female, to protect yourself and your partner against STDs, including acquired immune deficiency syndrome (AIDS). If you are heterosexual, it is your responsibility to protect yourself and your partner against unintended pregnancy (contraception). If your sexual partner objects to using disease and pregnancy protection, you must insist. Protecting yourself and your sexual partner is the most basic form of self-advocacy.

Sexuality Education

Every year, thousands of teens become pregnant or are infected with STDs because they haven't been educated about how to protect themselves or even about how their bodies work. Young people can become the victims of sexual harassment or sexual predators because they don't know what is happening to them until it's too late. Comprehensive, fact-based sexuality education gives young people accurate information about their bodies and tools for solid decision making. The Sexuality Information and Education Council of the United States (SIECUS) provides data and information about sexuality education in the United States and offers education to parents and communities. Statistics from SIECUS as of 2004 indicate that in states where fact-based sexuality education is either mandated or encouraged, rates of teen sexual intercourse, unprotected sex, pregnancy, STDs, and abortion are lower than nationwide rates. Many states require school districts to provide sexuality education in the form of "health" education, and in states that do not have such a requirement, districts are encouraged to do so through their public health departments.

The state of Maine has one of the country's most comprehensive sexuality education programs. Maine provides funding for sexuality education as part of its mandate. Tennessee is one of the most restrictive states, outlawing sexuality education unless the state department of public health has approved a school's program. In states such as New York, which requires schools to provide "health education," the law says that courses must include segments on abstinence-based sexuality education. Other states, such as California, which do not require sexuality education, do require education about

Many sex education books and websites provide detailed information about how to use condoms and dental dams, including: www.sexualityandu.ca (which has excellent illustrations), www.healthwise.org, www.teensource .org, and almost every college or university health service website, such as www.wellesley.edu/Health.

human immunodeficiency virus (HIV) and AIDS prevention "at least once" at the middle school or high school level. Many other states require that if sexuality education is taught, it must be based on the federally funded Title V "Abstinence-Only-Until-Marriage" program, which provides four dollars for every three dollars that the state allocates for such programs.

Shelby Knox is a teen who advocated for change by encouraging her community to offer comprehensive, fact-based sexuality education. Shelby, now a college student, was a religious fifteen-year-old Lubbock, Texas, high school sophomore who signed an "abstinence pledge" in 2001. Young people who sign such a pledge state that they will not have sexual intercourse until they are married. Most teens Shelby knew in her church youth group also signed the pledge. Shelby learned that Lubbock had one of the highest teen pregnancy and STD infection rates in her state.

The only sexuality education program available to Lubbock students, and to all other Texas public school students, was limited to the "Abstinence-Only-Until-Marriage" curriculum, which provides few medical facts. Shelby wondered how effective an "abstinence-only" sexuality education program could be, given her town's pregnancy and STD rates. She learned that Lubbock's gonorrhea rate was twice the national average. She was upset to see smart girls her own age "disappear" from high school when they got pregnant, forced to attend an alternative school. Shelby decided to focus on sex education as a school project. Over three years, she lobbied and made presentations to her local school board to persuade them that fact-based, comprehensive sexuality education was the way to lower Lubbock's sky-high teen pregnancy and STD rates.

A film team from IncitePictures, a partnership of independent documentary directors Marion Lipschutz and Rose Rosenblat, went to Lubbock in 2001 to document the impact of abstinence pledges and abstinence-only sexuality education. The filmmakers noticed how intent Shelby became about learning the

Shelby Knox. Photo by IncitePictures.

facts about sexuality in her community and began to focus on her and on her advocacy project. The result was *The Education of Shelby Knox*, an award-winning 2005 film that has been shown both in select theaters and on public television. To learn about local screening or television broadcast times for the film or to arrange to have the film shown in your area, visit the InsightPictures website: www.incite-pictures.com/shlbyknox/index.html.

Shelby's advocacy project in Lubbock did not result in getting fact-based sexuality education into the Lubbock public schools. Her advocacy project to help form a GSA at her school also was turned down. Nevertheless, because of the film, many people throughout the country have become aware of the need for responsible sex education. Shelby told a reporter for the

131

online magazine CampusProgress.org that she was not discouraged that her efforts weren't able to achieve her goal. "It's the teen voices that count the most in issues that relate to them," Shelby told CampusProgress.org. "All the adults in the world can tell a school board that they need sex education or that there needs to be gay–straight alliances to support high school students. But the students' voices are the most important. In the end, if you win or lose, you made a difference just by making the problem known."

Pregnancy and Disease Prevention

As we discussed in the previous section, there are many sexuality education programs that are based on the concept of no sex until marriage. Such programs are accurate when they say that the only sure method of preventing HIV/AIDS, STDs, and pregnancy is abstinence. However, most teens do not practice abstinence until marriage. Surveys and studies have shown for many years that young people start engaging in sexual behavior in middle school and that the majority of high school seniors have had sexual relations by the time they graduate. Reality-based sexuality education programs, like the kind Shelby Knox advocated for, encourage abstinence as the most effective method of contraception and disease prevention. However, reality-based sex education programs also provide information about effective contraception and disease prevention methods. Keep in mind:

- **Self-advocacy in a sexual relationship starts with being aware of what you can do to keep yourself safe.**
- **Self-advocacy in a sexual relationship also includes educating your partner about the methods of disease and pregnancy prevention, especially if your partner objects to using protection.**

The following section deals with methods of contraception, disease prevention, and alternatives that are available when an unintended pregnancy occurs.

Condoms and Dental Dams

For young people, condom use is the most readily available means of contraception and disease prevention. Condoms are inexpensive and portable and are highly effective if used properly. However, they do have expiration dates, and some materials are more effective than others are. Always use condoms before the expiration date on the package. Latex condoms are the most effective, so choose latex condoms rather than those made from other materials unless you have a latex allergy. Condoms are sold in almost every drugstore and in most corner stores and supermarkets. Condoms are equally effective when used in intercourse, oral sex, and anal sex.

Do you want to learn about your state's sexuality education requirements? Visit the National Coalition to Support Sexuality Education website, www.ncsse.org/mandates.html.

Dental dams are most effective in preventing disease in male-to-female and female-to-female oral sex. Dental dams are sometimes called the "female condom" and are often found in drugstores. Information about dental dams and female condoms, including instructions on how to make a dental dam from a condom, is available on the websites listed in the sidebar.

Using condoms and dental dams can prevent most STDs, and their use is effective in preventing HIV infection. However, there are many STDs that are not prevented by condom use. The scope of this book doesn't allow for a complete discussion of STDs and how to prevent or treat them. For more specific information about STDs, visit the websites listed and the TeenSource website at www.teensource.org/pages/3002/STDs.htm.

Contraceptives

If you are in a committed, exclusive heterosexual relationship, that is, you and your partner see only each other

Female condom. Female condoms are available over the counter.

and have not ever and do not plan to have sex with other people, you may decide together to use other forms of contraception to prevent unintended pregnancy. There are many contraception choices: oral contraceptives ("the pill"); Depo Provera, the contraceptive shot that protects against pregnancy for three months; the contraceptive patch; contraceptive foam or jelly; or a diaphragm used with contraceptive foam or jelly to prevent pregnancy. A new contraceptive implant has recently been approved by the Food and Drug Administration (FDA) that will provide extended pregnancy protection. Each of these methods of contraception has different rates of effectiveness and different side effects that you will want to research. There are also surgical means of contraception, including tubal ligation and vasectomy. However, surgery is a choice made primarily by adults and not by young people who might want to have children later in life.

You may have heard many old wives' tales about preventing pregnancy. Most of them are untrue!

- ◎ **Coca-Cola placed in the woman's vagina is not an effective method of contraception!**
- ◎ **Women can and do get pregnant when they are menstruating (having their period).**
- ◎ **Having the male withdraw his penis from the vagina before he ejaculates (has an orgasm or "comes") does not prevent pregnancy.**
- ◎ **The female's orgasm has no effect on whether or not she will get pregnant.**

The pill, the patch, the shot, and the diaphragm are, however, effective in most cases. All require a prescription to obtain, unlike condoms, contraceptive foam, and contraceptive jelly, which can be purchased at most drugstores.

Emergency Contraception

If you have had unprotected sexual intercourse and are afraid you might become pregnant, consider using emergency contraception. Emergency contraception, which is marketed in the United States as "Plan B," is an oral contraceptive given in specific doses and must be taken within seventy-two hours of unprotected sex to be effective. Emergency contraception, often called the "morning-after pill," is currently available only by prescription if you are under eighteen and over the counter if you are over eighteen. Many legislators are trying to persuade the FDA to allow over-the-counter sales of emergency contraception to younger women.

Your family doctor can do your examination and prescribe contraceptives for you. You may ask for a prescription for contraception or for the contraceptive shot or patch at the time of your examination. There are many clinics that offer low-cost physical examinationss. Some clinics offer low-cost prescriptions. Many insurance programs provide coverage for contraceptives. Many teens prefer the anonymity of a clinic setting, while others who feel comfortable discussing their sexual activity prefer the comfort of seeing a doctor they know and trust. You have the right to ask for and receive confidentiality (privacy) from your family doctor. Each state's laws about teen patient confidentiality differ slightly. However, if you are between ages twelve and eighteen, you should request and expect your doctor to keep your health issues, including your sexual behavior, confidential, even from your parents.

There are many health issues that can arise when young people engage in sexual activity. If you are sexually active, you should see a doctor (a gynecologist, a urologist, or a general practitioner) regularly to make sure you are sexually healthy.

Unintended Pregnancy

If you become pregnant and did not intend to become pregnant, you are probably upset, confused, and unsure of what to do next. Many people will have and will express their opinions about your pregnancy, including your doctor, your parent or guardian, your worship community, your friends, your school, and your sexual partner. You may want to keep and raise your baby but don't know how you can afford to take care of yourself and your child. You may want to continue your pregnancy but give your baby to another family to raise. Or depending on your feelings, your concerns, and your beliefs, you may decide that it is in your best interest to terminate, or end, the pregnancy. Pregnancy termination is most commonly known as abortion.

Abortion

In this book, we do not discuss the political or religious issues surrounding abortion. This section of the book simply states the medical and legal facts about abortion so that you can successfully advocate for yourself if you become pregnant. Because this book is written to help you advocate for yourself and achieve what you need in your life, we provide information about your legal rights to abortion and guide you to information about how to obtain an abortion or abortion alternatives.

Abortion can be done surgically or chemically. In the first trimester (the first three months) of pregnancy, the most common surgical method used is a vacuum aspiration, which takes only a few minutes and results in minimal discomfort. Surgical abortion after the first trimester is more complicated, and as the pregnancy progresses, the surgery requires more lengthy procedures that require longer recovery. Abortion after the first trimester may be illegal in your state.

Chemical abortion, also known as medical abortion or abortion by pill, involves the use of two different types of medication: one to terminate the pregnancy, the other to start contractions (cramps) in the uterus (womb). The medication you may have heard most about is mifepristone, which was discovered in France and prescribed there as RU486. The other medication that can be used in medical abortion is methotrexate. Both mifepristone and methotrexate must be used with another drug called a prostoglandin. Contractions caused by the prostoglandin will expel the pregnancy from your uterus.

Medical abortion is legal and can be prescribed by any physician in the country. However, although medical abortion is safe, it must be closely monitored by a medical practitioner to be sure the medication is taken properly and that the pregnant woman has expelled all the particles of the pregnancy from her body. Unmonitored medical abortion is not recommended and can lead to serious bleeding and other complications.

The Supreme Court decision known as *Roe v. Wade* (1973) declared abortion within the first trimester legal throughout the

United States. Since 1973, there have been several subsequent Supreme Court interpretations of the *Roe v. Wade* decision. Federal law requires states to fund abortions for impoverished women if the woman's life or health is at stake.

Individual states have passed laws that regulate abortion after the first trimester within their borders, including laws limiting the legal rights of minors to obtain an abortion without parental consent, laws requiring a waiting period between the initial appointment and the scheduled abortion, and laws that dictate whether state health program money can be used to fund abortion. Abortion remains legal throughout the country, but you will have to do research either in the library, online, or with your doctor to determine how and whether you will be able to access abortion in your state.

Many organizations such as Planned Parenthood, NARAL Pro-choice America, and the ACLU can assist you in finding out how to get an abortion. In some states, there is a process known as "judicial bypass" that provides young women with legal help to bypass the need for their parents to approve or be notified about their plans for an abortion. In such cases, the organizations mentioned here, and several others, have a group of attorneys who provide their services voluntarily to guide pregnant young women through the judicial process. Congress recently passed a law making it illegal to transport a minor across state lines (that is, from one state to another) for the purpose of assisting the minor in obtaining an abortion. Many states already have such a law.

To start your research, there is a summary of state abortion laws at www.hometown.aol.com/abtrbng/stablw.htm.

Keeping Your Baby

You may decide that you want to deliver and then raise your baby, either on your own or with your partner or your parents.

There are many organizations that will help you obtain health care and financial assistance during your pregnancy and immediately after you have your baby. If you are a member of a religious community, speak with your clergyperson to obtain information about what resources are available for pregnant teens who want to keep and raise their babies. Some religious organizations offer support and free health care for teens who decide to continue their pregnancies. Some state programs will pay for health care during pregnancy, provide a stipend of money to buy the things an infant needs, and provide financial assistance through at least the first several months of the baby's life.

Federal and state child welfare laws have become more restrictive in the past decade. Most laws now limit the number of months in their total lifetime that a mother and her child or children can be supported by the state. Many laws require that the mother accept job training and work at least a minimum number of hours per week or month. Many laws also limit the amount of financial assistance by the number of children a woman has: For example if the woman has two children, she will not receive an increase in her financial support if she has a third child.

Whatever your circumstances, if you decide to continue an unintended pregnancy, be sure to advocate for yourself to make sure that you have a healthy pregnancy and a healthy baby:

- See a doctor at least once each month during your pregnancy. The doctor will check to see that you have gained the right amount of weight, that your blood pressure is neither too high nor too low, and monitor the fetus's growth to be sure the baby is healthy. There are many clinics that will provide pregnancy services at low or no cost.
- If you are smoking, drinking alcohol, or taking any drugs (legal or illegal) *stop now*! Smoking, drinking, and drug use will have a terrible effect on your fetus as it grows in your uterus and will mean a lifetime of illness for your baby once it is born, including asthma, severe learning disabilities, and other ailments. If you are taking prescribed medications, talk to your doctor as soon as you know you are pregnant to determine whether the medicine will affect your baby.

◎ **Do research into how you will be able to support yourself and your baby once it is born. Find out if you can live in subsidized housing and receive a financial stipend for at least the first several months of your baby's life. You may be able to get financial support for childcare while you continue school.**

◎ **See chapter 9 about child support. If you are the baby's mother and will be raising your child, the baby's father is required to pay child support. If you are the baby's father and are going to raise your child, the mother is required to pay child support. Be sure you know your legal obligations before your baby is born.**

Adoption

You may wish to carry your baby to the full term of your pregnancy but not raise the baby yourself. When you give your baby to another person or couple to raise, you are placing your child for adoption. There are many more couples who want to adopt babies than there are babies available to be adopted. Many organizations, both secular and religious, throughout the United States and Canada offer services to young women who want to release their babies for adoption.

For your own emotional and physical health and for that of your baby, do your research about the organization that will provide health care for you and find a family to adopt your baby. While most adoption organizations are legitimate and caring, others are not. Find out about the history and reputation of the adoption organization. Some organizations will encourage you to get to know the adoptive parents who will raise your baby. Advocate for yourself and your baby:

◎ **Ask questions of the organization, including their rate of success in placing infants like your baby.**

◎ **Ask about the health care you will receive during your pregnancy and after you deliver your baby. Will you be able to choose your doctor and where you will give birth?**

◎ **Ask questions about the potential adoptive parents and their home. What is the family's history? Do they have other children? What is their home like? Will they be able to provide for your baby's education?**

There are many adoption agencies, and you deserve to use the right one. There are many sites to research about adoption, including www.adoptioninformation.com/Teen_pregnancy and www.gravityteen.com/adoption/news.cfm.

◎ Ask about the organization's policy on releasing your information to your baby when he or she is an adult and may want to contact you.

If you feel uncomfortable about any of the answers you receive to these questions, ask yourself if this is the organization with which you want to associate yourself and your baby.

TEEN DATING VIOLENCE

Self-advocacy is one of the best ways to stop teen dating violence. Whether you are the abused, the abuser, or a friend of either person, you can advocate to make the violence stop. Get the facts. Is what you are experiencing or observing dating violence? If it is, act quickly on behalf of your friend or yourself. Waiting can be dangerous.

Many young people, both male and female, have become involved in teen dating violence prevention projects. Help for Abused Women and their Children (HAWC), an organization dedicated to stopping domestic violence, has organized young people north of Boston to advocate for themselves and their peers. HAWC's outreach programs for youth, Lend UR Voice, for girls, and Boys for Leadership (B4L) meet weekly to learn and

(*continued*)

then pass on to others the warning signs of an abusive relationship, the cycle of violence, and how to help a friend who may be a victim of teen dating violence. Boys in the B4L program learned and passed on information about bullying, what it means to be a man, and about gender socialization.

Nicole Richone-Schoel, the Director of Community Outreach at HAWC, explains that in the summer, the program runs a summer camp in two inner cities and employs peer leaders in their teens. The teens, who have taken part in Lend UR Voice, teach younger kids about healthy relationships. "I think students should join Lend UR Voice because it's important for teens to understand and learn about violence and help many who are affected," said an eleventh grade Peer Leader.

Facts about Teen Dating Violence

- Teen dating violence crosses race, gender, and economic lines. Boys and girls are abusive in different ways:
  - Girls may yell, threaten to hurt themselves, pinch, slap, scratch, or kick;
  - Boys injure girls more severely and frequently; and
  - Some teen victims experience violence occasionally; others are abused more often, sometimes daily.
- Teens are at higher risk of intimate partner abuse than adults.
- Females ages sixteen to twenty-four are more vulnerable to intimate partner violence than any other age group—almost triple the national average.
- Approximately one in five female high school students reports being physically or sexually abused by a dating partner.
- Ninety-four percent of female victims between ages sixteen and nineteen are abused by a current or former romantic partner.
- Between 1993 and 1999, 22 percent of all homicides against females ages sixteen to nineteen were committed by an intimate partner.
- Youths involved in same-sex dating are just as likely to experience dating violence as youths involved in opposite-sex dating.
- Nearly one-half of adult sex offenders report committing their first sexual offenses before age eighteen.

(continued)

What to Look for

Be aware of danger signs in your own relationships and in those of your friends! Watch for any of the following. They may indicate you are in a violent relationship:

- He or she tells you he or she can't live without you.
- He or she breaks or hits things to intimidate you.
- Your weight, appearance, or grades have changed dramatically since you started seeing this person.
- He or she threatens to hurt himself or herself or others if you break up.
- He or she acts jealously, says jealous things, or exhibits aggressive behaviors.
- He or she pressures you into having sex or forces you to do sexual things you don't want to do by saying, "If you really loved me you would . . ."
- He or she is jealous and possessive about time you spend with friends.
- He or she is constantly checking up on you.
- He or she has severe mood swings or constant bad moods.
- He or she wants to limit your other school activities, so you can "be together more."
- You're frightened of him or her and worry about his or her reactions
- He or she wants your relationship to get serious too quickly

What to Do

Don't be afraid to speak up! Your or your friend's health and life could be at stake!

- Seek advice or training from an organization that addresses teen dating violence to learn how you can help ensure the victim's safety and stay safe yourself!
- Don't be silent about teen dating violence. Don't wait!
- If you suspect someone is a victim, encourage him or her to find help and tell someone he or she trusts.
- If you suspect someone is an abuser, tell him or her to tell someone he or she trusts and get help!
- Without being judgmental, listen, so you can find out what the problem is. Don't cut him or her off!

(continued)

- ◎ **Encourage the victim to speak up and speak out for himself or herself.**
- ◎ **Tell the victim he or she "deserves respect." Help him or her realize there is a problem.**
- ◎ **Tell the victim, "It's not your fault" and that there is never a reason to stay if he or she feels afraid, unhappy, or abused.**
- ◎ **Be prepared to find appropriate help for the victim.**
- ◎ **Keep in contact with the person so he or she doesn't feel alone.**
- ◎ **Contact an adult whom you trust and you feel can help.**
- ◎ **Help the victim make safety plans and help find a safe, public place to go.**

Adapted from American Bar Association National Teen Violence Prevention Initiative, 2006; KidsCounsel, 2006.

RESOURCES

American Bar Association Teen Dating Violence prevention program: www.abanet.org/unmet/toolkitmaterials.html
New York Civil Liberties Union, Information on Students' civil rights regarding sexuality: www.nyclu.org

The National Youth Advocacy Coalition
1638 R Street, NW, Suite 300
Washington, DC, 20009
www.nyacyouth.org/nyac/about.html

Sex, Etc.: www.sexetc.org/index.php.
Gender.org: www.gender.org/index.html.
SIECUS Community Action Kit: www.communityactionkit.org
National Coalition to Support Sexuality Education: www.ncsse.org/mandates.html
GLSN: Gay, Lesbian and Straight Education Network: www.glsen.org/cgi-bin/iowa/all/home.html

9 Legal Issues

Young people become involved in the legal system for many reasons, whether for juvenile justice matters (that is, criminal or delinquency), for civil matters (noncriminal, including, education, foster care, emancipation, and immigration), or because they must testify in a trial as a witness or a victim. Legal issues might arise in school (see chapter 5), at work, or if they arise outside of school, could have an effect on your school status. Some legal issues will require court intervention, while others won't. Many options could be available to you when you face legal issues in your life.

Whatever your reason for becoming involved in the legal system, you always can and should advocate for yourself. Do not underestimate the importance of your involvement. Be sure to get the facts, both about the law and about your individual situation. Inaccurate information can limit your options. "Street lawyers," such as friends who have been involved with the law, are not a reliable source of legal information. Keep this in mind: You are a legal minor until you reach age eighteen. Many laws have been written to protect you as a minor. That protection might feel troublesome to you at times. Until you reach eighteen, you may not vote, and without the permission of a parent, guardian, or other legally assigned adult, you may not sign contracts, consent to medical treatment, file suit, or get married, among many other actions, unless you become legally emancipated.

Many legal issues you encounter will require the assistance of an attorney licensed to practice in your state. Legal representation can be expensive, but most states fund legal defense programs to provide adults and young people with free legal help. Many states have charitable organizations, such as children's law centers that offer free (pro bono) assistance to children. Many law schools have law clinics or legal centers that specialize in legal advice for youths. In such cases, a law student, supervised by a professor who is a practicing attorney, may provide your representation. In other cases, a staff member at the law school who specializes in legal defense for youth will provide your representation.

In this chapter, we discuss issues and resources, how you are affected by an encounter with the legal system, and your legal rights regarding school, including if you become truant or homeless. We discuss your legal rights and issues as a pregnant or parenting teen, in immigration matters, when you're considering becoming an emancipated minor, and at work. We provide information on what to expect if you must testify in court. We also discuss your rights in the juvenile justice system and provide solid advice about how to self-advocate if you are arrested.

HOW YOU ARE AFFECTED

Your education, your ability to work safely, your freedom, and your future may depend on navigating the legal system successfully as a self-advocate with your attorney. Facing your legal issues with accurate information about your situation and your options will result in the best outcome. You will do much better in hearings and in court if you know your rights, are aware of how you can help yourself (and, even more important, how you can hurt yourself) through your behavior, and how self-advocacy and attention to the legal process can benefit your case and your future.

EDUCATION

Special Education

It is a federal mandate that schools must identify and provide services to students who require special education services. If your school does not do that for you or if the services the school provides are not adequately meeting your needs, the school is in violation of the law. If you are unable to receive satisfactory adjustments in your plan meetings at school, you are entitled to have your case mediated, and you are entitled to legal representation in that process.

Attorney Rebecca Vose, a staff attorney at the Juvenile Rights Advocacy Project (JRAP), a legal clinic program at Boston College School of Law, told us that education and individualized educational program (IEP) issues make up a large portion of the cases JRAP addresses on behalf of teens. Especially if you do not have an active parent advocate, find a children's law center, legal aid office, or law school clinic near you to be sure you receive the education you are entitled to. (See chapters 6 and 7 for details about your rights and how to advocate for yourself.)

Truancy

The laws in your state determine how many unexcused days you can miss school until you are considered truant. This could be as few as four days in a month or ten days in a year, no matter whether you miss them all at once or one at a time. Your state may consider you a "habitual truant" if you are under age sixteen and miss twenty days of school, unexcused, over the course of a school year.

Your local police department probably has a truant officer who tracks down students who are missing school. In some cases, the truant officer is allowed to insist that you come with him or her and will bring you to school. Once the school has declared that you are truant, it must follow a process that includes calling you and your parent or guardian to school for a meeting to discuss why you haven't been attending school. If your parent or guardian cannot or will not attend the meeting or if the school believes your parent or guardian isn't helping you to get to school each day, the school is usually required to refer your case to the court.

Some states have laws exempting students from attending school during times when their family's business requires them to help out, for example, during planting or harvest time. In almost every other case, however, working, whether in the family's business, to make money to support the family or to earn money to support independent living, is not an excuse for missing school. Most states have laws that require supervision, counseling, or monitoring for truant children—they may be called "Child in Need of Services" (CHINS) laws or "Youth in Crisis" laws. Once the court reviews your case, you may be assigned a probation officer to monitor your school attendance.

Truancy from school is serious. Depending on your and your parent or guardian's response to school or court intervention, you could be placed in juvenile detention for disobeying a court order to attend school. Truancy is often related to unmet special education needs, or to emotional issues the student has at school, at home, or in other aspects of life. Most schools approach attendance problems with an assessment of educational and other service needs. If you believe you are skipping school because the school is not providing the services you need, it's time to be an advocate for yourself. Read chapter 6 for more information about your rights to appropriate special education accommodations and for tips on how to advocate for yourself.

> Don't just stay home! Speak up! Contact a law center for children in your state. If you don't have online access, call your state's bar association for a referral. Many child law centers have youth advocacy programs that are dedicated to truancy prevention. They can help you know your rights and help you access the services you need in school.

Zero Tolerance and School Searches

School administrators committed to "safe school" policies act quickly when they suspect that students are involved with drugs, when students act violently or threateningly, or even if students make violent-sounding statements. (See chapter 5 for more information.) Zero tolerance usually means that students

Many organizations, including the American Civil Liberties Union (ACLU), are addressing zero-tolerance and school-search issues and are counseling and defending students whose school careers are threatened by suspension. See the ACLU website at www.aclu.org/studentsrights/ dueprocess/12782res20030717.html#attach. The University of Connecticut School of Law's Center for Children's Advocacy Teen Legal Advocacy Clinic (www.kidscounsel.org) is one of many children's law centers throughout the country that offer advice and assistance regarding school searches.

aren't given a second chance but can be suspended immediately for a first infraction of school rules. In most cases, schools must hold a hearing on your offense before suspending you. The school has the right to suspend you without notice (i.e., immediately) if administrators believe you are a danger to other students, but you have the right to a hearing as soon as possible after the suspension. If you receive a severe punishment (ten or more days of suspension) you have the right to be represented by a lawyer at the hearing. Here are some things to keep in mind in cases of zero tolerance and school search:

- It is best to cooperate with school officials in a search but be aware of and document (write down, in as much detail as possible) any behavior by school officials that you believe is excessive or in violation of your constitutional rights.
- Under the Fourth Amendment to the U.S. Constitution, school officials may only search you if they have reason to believe that *you* (not your friend or another person) have violated a school rule and that it is *likely* that the search will turn up something that is either illegal or against school rules.

◎ Searches may be conducted when reasonable evidence is present, such as the smell of cigarette smoke, the smell of alcohol on a student's breath, or the sound of gunfire that originates near a student.

◎ School searches must be done in a reasonable way, but school officials do not need a warrant to search your clothing, desk, or school locker, and the law does not require that a witness be present for the search.

◎ If you believe your search was conducted illegally, or that the zero-tolerance policy was enforced in violation of your civil rights, immediately contact your parents, the ACLU, or your local children's law center.

◎ Drug testing in schools has become a concern for many students. However, most appellate court decisions have given schools the right to test for illicit drug use. See chapter 5 for more on drug testing.

Suspension, Expulsion, Corporal Punishment, and Other Discipline

If you have been violent in school, have broken school rules, or have been involved in off-campus activities that are prohibited by school policy, you may face suspension for as little as a day or two or as long as several months. (See chapter 5 for more information.) Depending on your school's policies, you might not be allowed to keep up with class work at home while serving the suspension or be allowed to make up tests or reports you miss during the suspension.

Expulsion, being permanently barred from attending your school, is an even more powerful punishment. Many state laws prohibit expulsion from public schools, stating that expulsion violates students' rights to free education. Private schools, however, may use expulsion as the ultimate discipline. You may need legal representation to defend your rights if you are expelled from school. In some states, legal representation for expulsion is your right and might be available at no cost to you.

Only twenty-one states explicitly ban corporal punishment. States that allow it have established regulations about how and in what circumstances corporal punishment can be used. Most child advocates believe that hitting in school is inappropriate and does nothing to improve the learning environment. Immediately tell your parent or guardian if you are hit in school, and then contact your local ACLU or children's law center. If your state is one that does allow some form of corporal punishment, follow the steps in chapter 2 and self-advocate! Do your research and gather friends together to form a coalition with the aim of persuading your state to ban corporal punishment in school.

You should never be punished for violating a rule you weren't aware of because the school district didn't make its rules readily available to students. If this is the case in your school, advocate for yourself and your fellow students to be sure your school's rules are reasonable, are easy for students to understand, are publicly posted and published, and do not violate your constitutional rights. Chapter 5 addresses school rules in detail.

Homelessness and Your Education

The McKinney-Vento Homeless Assistance Act, which was passed in 1986, was reauthorized in 2001 to include education mandates for homeless children. The law provides a wide array of assistance and educational rights to children and youth in homeless situations. The act entitles young people to immediate enrollment in school despite their homeless status and prohibits placing homeless students in special or otherwise isolated classes. The law is important to the welfare of homeless and poor children, but it is underutilized and often ignored by school districts. Your public library may have documents on file regarding McKinney-Vento.

Homeless children are entitled to choose the school they want to attend and must receive transportation to their school of origin (that is, the school they attended before becoming homeless) if they want to continue attending that school. Homeless children are required to be enrolled in public school without immunization records if they are not available and

There are also a number of resources on the Internet to research the law and how its regulations can help you. Use a Google search to learn more, and be sure to visit the websites for the federal Department of Housing and Urban Development, www.hud.gov, the National Center for Homeless Education, www.serve.org/nche/m-v.php, and the National School Boards Association, www.nsba.org/site/doc_cosa.asp?TRACKID=&DID=33536&CID=164, among many others.

must have access to all the child services available in their school district. The law requires that any disputes that arise over the school system's handling of homeless children be mediated.

FOSTER CARE

The rights of children in foster care are extensive and complex. It is important that young people in foster care understand what they have the right to expect and the limits they will face regarding financial support and "aging out" of the foster care system. Many charitable organizations have been established to offer young people representation and resources beyond what their state's child welfare agency is able to provide. See chapter 10 for details and resources.

TEEN PARENTS

When you become a teen parent, issues immediately arise about paternity, custody, child support, and your right to continue

Even in paradise, teens have legal issues. On Kaua'i, Hawai'i, the Legal Aid Society of Hawai'i has started the Teen Parents and The Law project to help teen mothers and some teen fathers understand their rights in issues such as custody, visitation, child support, paternity, budgeting, landlord-tenant agreements, child abuse, neglect, family violence, and other matters. Gregory Meyers, the managing attorney for the society, says the program is "geared to help prevent child abuse and neglect, whether that child be the mother or offspring of the teen parent."

In 2003, the last full year of data available from state department of health officials, there were 107 births to teen mothers on Kaua'i. These are a few of the questions attorney Meyers answers and helps teen parents deal with on a daily basis: "Where do I go to get financial help for my baby girl? Is her father obligated to support her? How do I prove who her father is? Does it matter if his name is on the birth certificate? What is a temporary restraining order, and how can I protect my baby and myself from my abusive partner? My parents are telling me I cannot leave the house with my child; but it's my child, don't I have rights? My baby was born four weeks premature. What can I do to make sure she gets the nutrition and care she needs?"

If you are a teen parent with legal questions, contact the Legal Aid Society. For a branch near you, visit the national organization in charge of legal aid, the Legal Services Corporation, at www.lsc.gov.

your own education. Whether you are the mother or father of the baby, you become responsible for the care of another human being. Your child deserves to be supported and raised safely and responsibly. To raise your child responsibly, you might require the support of state and local organizations to help you be a successful parent. Many states provide financial and housing assistance for teen parents.

If you are a teen mother and the baby is living with you, the baby's father must pay child support, even if you are receiving state assistance. If you are a teen father and the baby is living with you, the baby's mother must pay child support. The birth mother will need to make a declaration of paternity and in

Get answers to the many questions you have about legal issues involved in pregnancy and parenting *before* the baby is born. Depending on your situation, you may need to actively self-advocate to get the support and assistance you need. The self-advocacy will be much easier to accomplish before you have a baby to care for.

some cases may need to prove paternity through DNA testing. The baby's father has the right to ask for DNA testing if there is a question about the paternity of the child. You must not be prohibited from attending public school as a result of your pregnancy and parenthood. See chapter 8 for more information about pregnancy discrimination.

Many child legal centers, including the University of Connecticut School of Law's Center for Children's Advocacy (CCA), have prepared useful materials about teen parental rights and responsibilities. Visit the CCA website at www.kidscounsel.org to access its brochures. Contact your local children's legal center for guidance and assistance in getting what you need to care for your baby and yourself.

IMMIGRATION

Becoming a U.S. citizen is a complicated process. Since the events of September 11, 2001, in which thousands of people were killed by terrorists from other countries, the U.S. government has been increasing barriers to entering the country and has been heightening surveillance of illegal immigrants. The debate about immigration has accelerated in Congress, and by the time this book is published, new laws may be implemented. If your parents came into the United States illegally or have stayed in the country beyond their visa period, your status will depend in part on whether you entered the country with them or were born here.

The American Immigration Law Foundation (AILF) is one of many charitable organizations established to help immigrants, including children, navigate the complicated laws and regulations on the road to citizenship. Their information-filled website is www.ailf.org. Thanks to a grant from actress Angelina Jolie, the American Immigration Lawyers Association, www.aila.org, started a program in 2005 called the National Center for Refugee and Immigrant Children, in conjunction with the U.S. Committee for Refugees and Immigrants. The Center will provide pro bono representation for unaccompanied children released in the United States. If you are a young person who is in need of representation or know of a friend who needs this kind of help, visit the AILA website at www.aila.org.

EMANCIPATION

If there is trouble in your home or with your foster care, you might decide you want to become emancipated, that is, no longer dependent on a parent, guardian, or the state, before you reach age eighteen. You are able to begin the process of emancipation at age sixteen or seventeen, depending on the laws of the state where you reside. To advocate for yourself in the emancipation process, first go to the library or online to research the laws in your state. Expect that the process will involve filing a form asking for emancipation with the appropriate court in your state—usually, juvenile court or probate court. The court will assign you either a hearing officer or a social worker to guide you through the process. At the emancipation hearing, the judge or magistrate will need to determine if you are an appropriate candidate for emancipation. Factors to be considered include: you are in a valid marriage; you are in the military; you are self-supporting; you no longer live with or are financially dependent on your parents; you will benefit from emancipation.

If you are successful in petitioning the court for emancipation, you will no longer need a parent or guardian's approval to get married, see a doctor, sign a lease, get a driver's license, attend college, or file a suit against someone, among other actions. However, while emancipation offers independence, it also requires a great deal of responsibility. No programs are set up to help emancipated minors adjust to their new freedom, either financially or in other ways. You will become entirely responsible for supporting yourself, which includes paying rent, buying your own food, and paying for your own health care.

There may be better ways to improve your living situation than filing for emancipation. Talk with your social worker or another trusted adult, contact your state's children's law center, and weigh the pros and cons. You may be able to access financial and educational support to help you improve your life.

WORK

Each state's laws about juvenile work requirements vary. However, U.S. Department of Labor (DOL) standards for child labor set age fourteen as the minimum working age and limit the hours worked by minors under sixteen. Federal and state child labor laws cover even emancipated minors (under age eighteen). The U.S. Fair Labor Standards Act views certain types of employment as hazardous for minors, including those involving operating heavy machinery and those involving driving. The major exception to all child labor laws is for family farms: all youth, regardless of age, are allowed to perform any form of labor when employed by their family on the family farm. In cases where state laws and federal laws overlap, the law that is more restrictive about protecting youth will apply.

Despite the many safeguards put in place by federal and state laws, young people continue to be injured on the job because they are forced to work longer hours than is safe, to

The DOL website offers information on state child labor laws and provides links to each state's laws: www.dol.gov/elaws/esa/flsa/cl/default.htm. Most states require that youth under age sixteen obtain an employment certificate or "working papers" before becoming employed, though some states require certification for youth under age eighteen. You can get information about how to get employment certificates at www.dol.gov/esa/programs/whd/state/certification.htm.

perform tasks that are too dangerous for them, or because they are not adequately supervised. In Massachusetts alone, 3,723 teens were injured on the job between July 1993 and June 2003. In 2004, 134 youth deaths occurred in the workplace nationwide. The majority of those injuries occurred on the job in restaurants, on construction sites, at recreation sites, and in factories. If you believe your employer does not adequately protect your safety at work, it's time to self-advocate. Do your research. Find out, using the library or the links on the DOL website, what child labor protection laws are in effect in your state. If the work you are being asked and expected to do violates the law, follow the steps in chapter 2.

Take notes and document what you do at work, how many hours you work, and what the law states. Then speak with your employer. Calmly and politely, explain what your situation is, and suggest how it could be improved. If you aren't satisfied with your employer's response, call your state legislator; his or her phone number will be listed in the phone book. Don't hesitate! The child labor protection laws are written to keep you from being injured or worse.

In 2006 in Massachusetts, teens who were part of Teens Lead at Work, the Massachusetts Coalition for Occupational Safety Health's (MassCOSH) youth division decided to advocate for stricter child labor laws in their state. The teens worked with their local state legislator to help write a bill that requires adult supervision of all youth workers after 8 p.m., limits the hours teens may work, and adds other safeguards for teens in the workplace. Read more on the MassCOSH website at www.masscosh.org.

TESTIFYING IN COURT

If you are the victim of a crime or a witness to one, if you have been involved in domestic violence and are seeking a restraining order or if you are involved in a civil suit, you could be called to testify in court. Testifying means answering questions under oath. *Under oath* means that you promise to tell the truth.

Testifying can feel intimidating. Because the U.S. legal system is based on the assumption that a person is innocent until proven guilty, the defendant has many rights to ensure that he or she receives a fair trial. The defendant's attorney, who acts on his or her behalf, has the right to confront witnesses in an attempt to show a judge or jury that the witnesses' testimony is untrue or unreliable. It is normal to feel worried or concerned about testifying in court. If you are the one who will bring the facts to light in court, you may feel that you are under a lot of pressure. It may help you to feel less stressed out to think about how important it is to help achieve justice in your case.

There are many rules and regulations that have been put in place to protect young witnesses. In a criminal case, the prosecutor will be an assistant district attorney. Many states will provide you with an advocate called a *guardian ad litem* who will represent you during the trial period. The guardian ad litem can ask the judge to limit the time you are expected to testify, to allow your parents to be with you when you testify, or even to testify on a closed-circuit camera from a separate room. Many states also have victim/witness advocates who can keep track of how the legal professionals are treating you and can serve as a sounding board for your concerns. The advocate can tell you all you will need to know about the trial process.

There are many ways to self-advocate if you will be testifying in court:

- If you are feeling extremely anxious and upset about testifying, ask to see a therapist who can help you sort through your feelings.

- Ask the victim/witness advocate to explain in detail how each part of the trial process works. Your advocate can give you information about who will be in court, what each of those people does, and what to expect at each stage of the trial.

- Concentrate on telling the truth. Most prosecutors advise against actually rehearsing your testimony out loud. Nevertheless, it will help you to mentally review the details of the case, especially what happened to you, how you felt, and what you saw. It is the defense attorney's job to try to get you to make a mistake. It is harder to make a mistake if you are telling the truth.

- When you are testifying, don't be afraid to say you are confused or that you don't know the answer to a question.

- Make sure the lawyers and your advocates know about your schedule at school and at home. If you are an athlete who needs to be at games or a match, if you know an important test will be given on a certain day or if a school or family trip has been planned that could coincide with the trial, let the adults in charge know as soon as possible.

No matter what the final legal decision, it is the right thing to do to tell the court the truth. You deserve all the assistance you can get to support you in the process of testifying.

For more information on testifying, contact the National Center for Missing and Exploited Children at 1-800-843-5678 or at www.missingkids.com.

JUVENILE JUSTICE AND DELINQUENCY

There are many laws, and many ways to break them. Teens, who are prone to take risks, often place themselves in harm's way of the law by testing their limits. When an arrest is the result, adequate legal representation is critical. The complications that arise from being arrested are serious and life affecting. You may find yourself arrested for attending a party in a home where alcohol is being served or as a passenger in a car when the driver has been drinking. You may be arrested because you violated the law or because you are suspected of violating a law. You may be declared delinquent and taken into custody if you and your parent or guardian become angry or violent with each other and the police are called to intervene. Detention or jail time may face you as punishment for the offense.

Do *not* underestimate the serious impact a jail sentence will have on your future!

The laws against drug use, drug possession, and drug sales and distribution are strict, and conviction means serious punishment. A drug possession conviction, especially when it involves sale and intent to distribute, means you face long mandatory prison sentences. An arrest on drug charges is as serious as an arrest for violent crime.

"I was in trouble once before and didn't know what was happening to me. It was scary to be in a criminal courtroom, and I was lucky to get probation. This time, I got arrested with a lot of other kids just for being in a house where kids were drinking. I wasn't drinking at all! I found the Children's Law Center, and they really helped me figure out what to do to help myself out. Most of the other kids came to court in cutoffs and T-shirts, but I was neat and clean. The judge asked me what happened, and because I mentally rehearsed it first, I could tell my side of the story. My case was dismissed!"—Julian, age seventeen

The most important aspect of juvenile justice and delinquency for you will be the way you advocate for yourself in the justice system. If you take the process seriously, educate yourself about the law, and communicate clearly and directly with your attorney, your outcome is more likely to be successful. See the sidebar "If You Are Arrested" for details on how you can self-advocate.

WHAT YOU CAN DO

Self-advocacy in legal matters may seem difficult. However, there are many legal resources for young people.

Take a Course

Public schools can benefit by associating with area law schools. For example, Boston College Law School supports a

"Street Law" course for students at Brighton High School near Boston, using a curriculum developed by the Georgetown University School of Law. More than seventy law schools throughout the country now offer a Street Law course to high schools in their community. In Connecticut, Hartford High School students have regular visits from KidsCounsel, a program of the University of Connecticut Law School. Students have the opportunity to ask practicing attorneys and law students questions about legal issues.

Your school may already offer a Street Law course or regular connections with law students and practicing lawyers. If so, you can take advantage of the opportunity to learn the facts about laws that affect you. If your school doesn't have a law program, find out if there is a law school in your community or

TEEN COURT

You might want to learn about the legal system by taking part in a hands-on program known as teen court. As of 2006, there were nearly one thousand teen courts or youth courts in the United States, with programs that follow a variety of models. Teen court programs are designed as educational tools for youthful offenders and their peers. If there is a teen court program near you, you could be trained to serve as a peer juror, judge, defense or prosecuting attorney, or another court officer.

If you are a teen who has broken the law in an area where there is a teen court, you may opt, with parental approval, to be judged and sentenced by peers rather than take the chance of acquiring a criminal record. Sentences handed out by teen courts usually involve community service, restitution, and some form of counseling. In some teen court programs, a peer mentor is assigned to counsel the defendant post-sentencing to help the youth in trouble live up to the conditions of his or her sentence.

To learn more about teen courts and about how you can advocate to start one in your area, visit the American Bar Association website at www.abanet.org/publiced/youth/teencourts.

in a nearby city. If the law school offers a Street Law curriculum or another legal assistance or information program, follow the steps in chapter 2 and advocate for a course to be offered at your school.

Research at the Library or Online

Your local library should have copies of the laws of your state. Because the books are probably reference books, you won't be able to take them home, but you will be able to take notes while you're in the library on the state laws that affect your situation. Many states have established comprehensive, organized websites that make it possible to access all the laws of the state, including updates and revisions. Many legal organizations offer websites with valuable legal information for young people, including schools of law, the ACLU, and the American Bar Association. See the Resources list at the end of this chapter to start your information gathering, and do a Google or Wikipedia search to continue researching specifics about your situation.

Free Representation

In juvenile justice cases, if you are estranged from your parents or guardian, or if you or your parents cannot afford to hire a lawyer, your local bar association's legal defense program can provide a lawyer for you. In some states, children in foster care are assigned a lawyer to represent them, while in other states, children in foster care are not entitled to legal representation paid for by the state. There are children's law centers (sometimes known as youth law centers or centers for youth law) in several states. The National Law Center on Homelessness and Poverty is dedicated to making sure that homeless and indigent students receive all the rights and opportunities they are entitled to under the law. The United Way in your area may provide legal representation if you can't afford it. No matter what the situation in your state, it is possible to find good quality, low-cost, or free representation if

IF YOU ARE ARRESTED

Attorney Barbara Kaban, Director of Research and Policy for the Children's Law Center of Massachusetts, told us in a 2006 interview that young people who have been arrested can and should self-advocate. To successfully advocate for themselves in the legal system, teens should know the following things about their rights when they are arrested.

Immediately after the Arrest

Any statement you make can be used against you in court. You will be upset and confused when you are arrested. Never answer questions from the police about the incident for which you've been arrested until you've spoken to an attorney. To get as much information from you as possible, it is legal for police to lie to you while they are asking questions after your arrest. For example, they may tell you that a friend has already confessed or that your friend has blamed you for the incident for which you've been arrested. Or they may say, "Just tell us the truth and you can go home."

Jail cell. The entrance to a juvenile holding cell in Marblehead, Mass.

"If they have enough evidence to arrest you, they have enough evidence to hold you" [at the police station until parents arrive or someone pays bail], attorney Kaban says. "Keeping quiet never gets you held. The best thing is not to agree to answer questions. Kids' parents also do not understand that any statement you make can be used against you in court, and they will say to the kid, 'tell the truth and they'll let you go.'" In the confusion and upset following the arrest, the best thing is to stay silent and tell your attorney what happened in your first meeting.

In the Court System

"The case is about you, so you have to be [proactive]," attorney Kaban says. The attorney–client relationship, she says, is critical to the success of a legal case. "The

(continued)

best thing kids really can do is talk through their attorney, and the more information the attorney has, the better. Their attorney's role is to be the child's voice in court—the only way the attorney can do that is to know what the child wants.

"I always tell kids that if you're not understanding what's happening to you, make sure you do understand, and ask questions. This case is about you and your life. It's not always easy because a lot of attorneys are not good at communicating. Self-advocacy is important in the legal system, and especially the juvenile justice system—teens have a right to know what's going on in their case. There are decisions the attorney is going to make [about how to proceed with the case], but some decisions only the kid can make, like whether to plead out [plead guilty for a lesser sentence] or go to trial. They can only make those decisions if they're understanding what their attorney is saying and doing."

Communicating with your attorney can be difficult, for many reasons. "The problem that occurs for a lot of kids is they don't know how to contact their attorney, and they need to know how to reach their attorney," attorney Kaban says. "One thing the kid can do about it is, they have to ask for a card from the attorney. All attorneys have cards, and they should take at least one every time they have an appointment. That way they'll have the information with them to contact their attorney."

If You Are Unhappy with Your Attorney

Attorney Kaban is frank in saying that communication problems can be due to the attorney: "Some attorneys are good, but some are terrible. If your attorney isn't communicating with you, you have to keep records. Date everything. It doesn't need to be fancy, just keep a log." The log can simply be notes on a piece of paper, as long as there are records that can show the judge what has happened between you and your attorney. In some states, judges will not listen to a young person in court and require that attorneys do all the talking for a teen. However, if you are having a problem with your attorney, you can let the judge know this in other ways. "A kid can say, [to the judge] I've tried to call my attorney on such and such a date, and never got a response," attorney Kaban says. If you are in a courtroom with a presiding judge who does not want juveniles to speak in court, you "can give a note with the request and with your log to a court officer." Attorney Kaban says there are "simple things kids can do for themselves" in the court system. "Be a good advocate for yourself. You have to understand what the court system is about. For example, it *does* matter how you are dressed—don't come into court wearing gang colors, for example. Judges aren't stupid."

Self-advocate and speak up: You are your lawyer's client, whether his or her fee is paid by you or your parents, by the state, or by a charitable organization. To represent you successfully, you must be honest with your lawyer, and your lawyer must listen to you to understand your information and your specific needs.

you do the research and advocate for yourself. Barbara Kaban, the director of research and policy for the Children's Law Center of Massachusetts, advised in 2006 that teens should take notes and be persistent with their lawyer. (See Sidebar, "If You Are Arrested.") Most important: Don't give up! You can change your life and save your future by self-advocating.

RESOURCES

- American Bar Association Center on Children and the Law: www.abanet.org/child/home2.html
- American Immigration Law Foundation: www.ailf.org
- American Immigration Lawyers Association: www. aila.org
- American Civil Liberties Union: www.aclu.org/studentsrights/ dueprocess/12782res20030717.html#attach
- The Children's Law Center: www.childrenslawcenter.org
- Children's Law Center of Massachusetts: www.clcm.org
- U.S. Department of Housing and Urban Development: www.hud.gov
- National Center for Homeless Education: www.serve.org/ nche/m-v.php
- National Center for Missing and Exploited Children: 1-800-843-5678; www.missingkids.com

- National School Boards Association: www.nsba.org/site/doc_cosa.asp?TRACKID=&DID=33536&CID=164

- University of Connecticut School of Law Center for Children's Advocacy: www.kidscounsel.org

- Boston College Law School: www.bc.edu/schools/law

- Department of Labor: www.dol.gov/elaws/esa/flsa/cl/default.htm

- Legal Services Corporation: www.lsc.gov

- Massachusetts Coalition for Occupational Safety Health's (MassCOSH): www.masscosh.org

- National Council for Occupational Safety and Health: www.coshnetwork.org

- Youth Law Center: www.ylc.org

10 Foster Care

There are as many reasons why children are placed in foster care as there are families. The bottom line, though, is this: If your biological or adoptive family cannot safely and responsibly care for you and your needs, you and/or your siblings will be placed in your state's care.

You are not alone! There are more than a half million children in foster care all across the United States. Every state has an agency responsible for providing services to foster children. The agency may be called the department of social services, the department for children and families, or something similar. In most cases, the state agency will place you in a family setting known as a foster home. However, because there has been and remains a significant shortage of appropriate foster homes throughout the United States, it may be necessary that you or your siblings be placed in a group residential setting.

Being placed in foster care is not your fault! It is emotionally painful to be taken from your parents and placed in foster care, even if your home situation was inappropriate and dangerous. Like most children in foster care, you probably will continue to love your parents even if you have been abused or neglected by them. You will find it wrenching to be separated from them and will hope that your family can be reunited. Most children who enter foster care suffer from emotional upset. It's normal to feel sad, angry, lonely, and helpless after being separated from your parents.

It's important to know this: If you are a child in foster care, you have many rights. If any issues arise while you are in foster care, including if your foster placement does not meet your needs, you can successfully advocate for yourself and get your situation improved. Self-advocacy in foster care may sometimes be difficult and may require persistence on your part, but by learning how to negotiate the foster care system, you will be better able to access the care, treatment, services, and funding that are your rights.

Both the state where you live and the foster family or group home where you are placed have many responsibilities. As temporary or replacement parents, they must adequately educate you, house and clothe you, provide you with health care, and keep you safe. They must allow you to maintain your relationships with your family and your friends and make it possible for you to continue attending religious services in your own faith.

In foster care, many issues arise between child and foster family, between child and social worker, between child and birth parents, and within the community where the child lives and goes to school. In this chapter, we discuss how you are affected by foster care, your rights as a foster child, and what you can do to advocate for yourself to be sure you receive the housing, education, health care, nurturing, and other opportunities you deserve. We also provide a list of resources to use, as well as a sidebar about special programs for foster kids that offer grants and funding, including money to finance your education and training once you leave foster care.

HOW ARE YOU AFFECTED?

The state will place you in a foster home or group residence that has been inspected by the child welfare agency in charge of foster care. Many foster families care for more than one child at a time, but a private home where a foster parent cares for two or more foster children is not considered a group home. A group home is often a dormitory-like building where many children are supervised by twenty-four-hour staff, including a residence supervisor, who is in charge of the home, and other staff members who might serve as counselors, tutors, house masters, or cooks, or perform other duties. The placement must be physically safe, clean, and provide adequate sleeping quarters for the foster children residing there. It is acceptable to have children share a bedroom, whether in a private home or a group residence.

Most states require that potential foster parents take a series of courses to educate them about the special needs of foster children. Foster parents receive payment, in the form of a daily stipend, to cover the cost of housing, feeding, and caring for you. They also receive small, but regular, additional payments to purchase clothing for you. The daily stipend and clothing stipends are modest; few foster parents take care of children because they want to get rich. In a group home, the stipend helps to pay the cost of running the house, but you are entitled to the entire amount of any additional stipend, such as those for clothing.

The state agency responsible for your care will assign you a social worker or caseworker who will counsel you, listen to your questions and concerns, and monitor your education, health care, and housing needs. Your social worker will be your legal guardian while you are in foster care. Your social worker is the person you will contact when you have issues with your birth parents, your foster home, your school, your emotional well-being, or your health care. Your state agency may also provide you with an attorney who will assist in preparing your treatment plan and represent your rights while you are in foster care. In states where an attorney is provided to you, it is important to maintain contact with your attorney, to have his or her contact information, and to be sure he or she understands and correctly represents your wants and needs. In states where an attorney is not provided for you, it is a good idea to contact a children's law center in your state or a law school that offers pro bono (free) legal representation. See chapter 9 for more information.

YOUR FOSTER HOME OR GROUP HOME

It is never easy to live with strangers, whose household, habits, food, and rules may be different from what you are used to. That is especially true if you are placed in a group residence with many other children. When you are taken from your birth family's home and placed in a foster home or group home, everything will feel strange at first. Your social worker and your foster family or residence supervisor should be aware of how upset and awkward you feel about such major changes in your life.

You will be required to follow the rules in your foster home or group home. The rules may be strict, but they must also be appropriate for your age. Rules cannot involve punishment that includes threatening, frightening, mocking, swearing at you, or hitting you. If this ever happens to you or if you are hurt or feel threatened by your foster parents, their children, their guests, by your residence supervisor, or by other children in your group home, immediately contact your social worker. It may be necessary to move you out of that foster placement for your safety.

> If you are feeling emotionally troubled as a result of the problems in your family, about the separation from your family, about the adjustment to foster care, or all of these issues, you deserve to receive therapy to help you with your feelings. Speak to your social worker to make sure you receive professional counseling on a regular basis.

Siblings

Whenever possible, the state will place you in the same foster home with your siblings. If it is not possible to find a home that can take all of you, your foster parents or group home staff and your social worker must make it possible to contact and visit your siblings regularly to avoid further disruption in your life.

Religion

Even if your foster parents' religion or culture is different from yours, they must provide you with an opportunity to go to your own house of worship. They cannot force you to attend the house of worship in their faith if it is different from yours or force you to take part in religious observances that are in conflict with your own beliefs.

Language

Your foster family or residence supervisor must allow you to speak the language with which you were raised. However, if your foster care provider's primary language is English, it will make sense to speak to him or her in English, both to make sure your needs are understood and to fit in as best you can.

Food

You may request that the food you are served include some foods that are familiar to you. However, foster parents and group homes are not required to do this. They must give you healthful food, not just foods you like. You may want to offer to cook for your foster family or make a meal at your group home or to cook with them to teach them how to prepare the kind of food you love. They may love it, too!

Negotiating

If you have issues with your group home or foster parents about rules, how you are treated, or other aspects of your life in the home, try talking things over to reach a compromise. Follow the beginning steps in chapter 2, remembering to know your audience. Remember that, just as it is difficult for you to adjust to a new living situation, it is difficult for the foster family or the group to adjust to a new and different person in their lives. Even if you are feeling emotional, don't yell. Find a calm time and ask politely to speak about your needs.

If having a discussion with your foster parent or residence supervisor doesn't make life in the foster placement go more smoothly, speak up about it to your social worker. Your social worker will try to negotiate adjustments that you and your foster family can all agree on. Sometimes all it takes to improve a situation is another viewpoint, and your social worker can help both sides see how to make the situation better for everyone.

Sexuality

If you are or believe you may be gay, lesbian, bisexual, transgender, or questioning, it is a good idea to be honest and up front with your caseworker about your sexual orientation or questioning. Not all foster homes are accepting and supportive of gay teens and that might prove uncomfortable for both you and them or even dangerous for you. Your caseworker can both maintain your confidentiality about your sexuality and make sure that your placement is a healthy one for you. If you find yourself in a foster placement that is a bad fit because of your sexuality, call your social worker immediately.

Moving

Most social service agencies will try to avoid moving you frequently. Each move is disruptive to you and has an effect on your sense of stability and belonging. Each move means another set of adjustments to another set of rules and expectations and often, to another school system and different friends. Sometimes, however, you will not be able to adjust to each other, even if both sides try to get along, and a move

Emergency removal from a foster placement isn't easy. You may think it's easier to put up with a difficult situation than to disrupt your life with a move. Don't hesitate! Moving is better than staying in a dangerous situation! Your safety and well-being are your social worker's primary concern, and they should be your primary concern as well.

cannot be avoided. Your social worker will do his or her best to make the move a positive one for you. If a foster placement feels dangerous to you, if you are not being treated well or fear for your health in any way, contact your social worker immediately, even at night or on weekends. You may need to be placed in a temporary home until an appropriate long-term placement can be found.

Education

You are entitled to, and are required to, have your education continue uninterrupted while you are in foster care. Most state agencies will try to place you in your same community when you enter foster care, unless remaining in the community would prove dangerous for you. Even if your foster placement is in another community, many states give you the opportunity to stay in your same school, again, unless that would prove dangerous to you.

If it is necessary that you change schools, your new school will be required to provide whatever special education services or disability accommodations you require. You deserve to learn at your best possible level. Your social worker will be your educational advocate and will review and approve all education plans recommended by your school. Your foster family may want to take part in your education plan meetings to help you achieve your educational goals. Read through the "What You Can Do as a Foster Child" section about how to keep track of your school records if you move from one school to another.

"I can be successful, even if I am a foster child. Being in the court system has basically given me another chance. I have a lot of supportive people cheering me on while I complete my life as a foster child. They share with me that I have made a difference in their lives, just seeing my level of healthiness and responsibility grow."—Angela, High School Senior, Los Angeles

Treatment Plan

Once you enter foster care, the state social services agency will talk with you, your parents, your foster parents, your teachers and school administrators, and your medical providers to come up with a "treatment plan" for you. Some agencies may call the treatment plan by a different name. In almost every case, your treatment plan will be put together with your needs and well-being the primary goal. You can expect that the treatment plan will be a record, in writing, of the services you need and should receive while you are in foster care. Your treatment plan may also detail what actions your parents must take to regain custody of you (reunification). If the state decides to terminate your family's parental rights, your treatment plan may include adoption as a goal. The plan should be reviewed regularly to update any changes that are needed.

Your treatment plan should be shared openly with you—after all, it's about you, and it will affect your future. If you don't have a copy of your treatment plan, ask for one. If there is anything in your treatment plan that you don't understand, ask to have it explained. If there are parts of your treatment plan that you disagree with, ask why each decision was made.

If you would like parts of your treatment plan changed, follow the steps in chapter 2 to begin a self-advocacy process for yourself. Your social worker is your advocate in dealing with your treatment plan. However, to be sure you receive the services and attention you require be aware of your right to self-advocate.

CONTACT AND VISITS WITH YOUR BIOLOGICAL FAMILY

Depending on your individual situation, it may be the state child welfare agency's eventual goal to return you to your parents' custody (this is usually called *reuniting* or *reunification*.) However, your parents will have to meet strict requirements before you can be reunited with them. For example, if your birth parents are addicted to alcohol or other drugs or are incarcerated, the state may require that they enter treatment to recover from their addiction, serve out their sentence, or enter a program for rehabilitation. In most cases, your parents will have to prove that they are clean and sober, that they can support you and provide for your needs, and that your living situation will be safe.

If you have been abused or neglected by your birth parents, the state will require that they receive counseling and education on parenting in addition to any prison sentence they may receive for the abuse. To determine when and whether it is safe for you to return to their care, the state and your social worker will do a thorough investigation, which will probably include supervised visits between you and your birth parents.

KINSHIP PLACEMENTS

The state may try to minimize the disruption you feel when your parents aren't able to safely care for you by placing you in the home of family members or close friends. These are called kinship placements. Foster parents who are also your family members or close friends must meet the same standards as unrelated foster parents: Their homes must be safe and must provide appropriate sleeping arrangements for you. Just like unrelated foster parents, the family members or friends must be educated about the special needs and fears of foster children so they can understand what you are going through and help you adjust.

YOUR RIGHTS IN FOSTER CARE

Each state's laws differ slightly regarding the rights of children in foster care. In some states, such as Connecticut and Massachusetts, all foster children are assigned an attorney whose job it is to advocate for the child in educational, custody, and other matters. Other states neither assign an attorney nor consider it a foster child's right to have legal representation. If your state does not provide you with an attorney when you enter foster care, you may obtain an attorney through one of many charitable organizations dedicated to providing legal representation for children. See chapter 9 for resources to investigate.

No matter what your state's individual laws, you have these rights as a foster child:

- You have the right to contact with your family and friends, as long as that contact will not hurt you.
- You have the right to practice your own religion.
- You have the right to your own money, whether you earn it or have money given to you as an award or a gift.
- You have the right to be treated with dignity and respect.
- You have the right to be safe.

- You have the right to adequate living conditions, including healthful meals, well-fitting and clean clothing, and privacy appropriate to your age.
- You have the right to education and to any special services and accommodations you require to learn.
- You have the right to health care and dental care.
- You have the right to know the details of your treatment plan.
- You have the right to a social worker who is accessible to you, who listens to what you need and want, and who acts on your behalf.
- You have a right to have your social worker's phone number, an emergency number, and regular visits from your social worker.
- You have a right to assistance that prepares you for independent living when you age out of foster care.

In addition, many advocates believe that foster children must be provided with comprehensive sexuality education and guidance as their bodies change during puberty. Because many foster children have been the victims of sexual abuse, attention to questions about their sexuality is essential, and therapy for those troubled by their abuse is crucial. If you are being denied your rights, if your questions are not being answered adequately, or if you are having a serious problem in your foster home, it is critically important to speak up and ask for what you need.

> "I feel that more teen youth need to step up and take a 'piece of the pie.' Youth complain because of the overloaded caseloads, but they can become more independent by using the resources provided to them in their environment. More youth need to advocate for themselves."—Chelz, seventeen, in Michigan foster care more than three years

PARENTING TEENS IN FOSTER CARE

If you are a teen in foster care and have a baby, there may be state services available to provide for day care, health care, and even financial payments to provide food, clothing, and diapers for your baby. In some states, the social services agency in charge of foster care will pay for necessary baby items, such as a crib, stroller, and car seat. Social services can also arrange for adoption, if you are unable or unwilling to raise your baby yourself. See chapter 8 for information about pregnancy options and about the use of contraceptives to prevent further pregnancies if you remain sexually active.

INDEPENDENT LIVING

In some cases, teens in foster care are allowed to prove that they are mature enough to live on their own, perhaps in their own apartment, rather than remaining in a foster home or in a group residence. Each state's regulations vary on how, at what age, and whether the agency responsible for foster care can consider supporting you when you live on your own. Living on your own in this way differs from becoming a legally emancipated minor because the state will continue to provide you with income and support. See chapter 9 for information about emancipation.

To advocate for yourself to live independently, do your research in the library and online about the process required in your state. Using the steps in chapter 2, organize your thoughts and put together your reasons for wanting to live on your own. Start a discussion with your social worker. If your state provides you with a lawyer while you are in foster care, schedule a meeting with your lawyer to start the process. If not, find a child law center in your area to discuss the requirements in your state. Researching how to obtain permission from the state to live independently may be a good way for you to prepare to deal with the aging out process, even if you decide to remain in a foster placement.

Attorney Stacey Violante Cote, Director of the Teen Legal Advocacy Clinic Center for Children's Advocacy at the University of Connecticut School of Law, told us in 2006 that it can be upsetting and confusing to make choices about your living situation when you are in foster care. "I get lots of questions from kids about 'living options,'" attorney Violante Cote says. "A kid will come to me and say, 'I'm thinking of running away,' or 'I got kicked out last night,' 'I want to be emancipated,' or that he wants to live independently," attorney Violante Cote says. "I get a lot of kids who come to me thinking they have just one option of what they can do. They may think about emancipation or a transfer of guardianship. I ask them to ask themselves 'which legal options do I have?'" With her knowledge of the foster care system, attorney Violante Cote can review each possible option and what the benefits and complications are of each option. "Then," she says, "I can help the teen determine which option fits for them." For information about the University of Connecticut program, visit www.kidscounsel.org.

AGING OUT

Most states stop providing foster care and financial support for young people when they reach eighteen—this is called aging out of the foster care system. Some young people are anxious to reach eighteen and become independent. Others would prefer to have the state continue providing housing and educational assistance for them while they attend college or while they further their education in other ways. Many advocates for children and youth believe that eighteen is too young for a teen to be aged out of foster care and are lobbying to establish the age of majority, twenty-one, as the national standard.

If your eighteenth birthday is approaching, it's time to do your research and find out how you can best advocate for yourself. If you're a younger teen, it's not too early to learn about your options, whether you expect to live as an independent young person or want to continue in the foster care system. Your state is required to provide you with some form of preparation for independence. If you haven't received such services, ask your social worker about the help you are supposed to receive and when you can expect to receive that help. Independence can come as an expensive and unpleasant shock if you haven't planned adequately or have a social

IMPROVE YOUR LIFE IN AND AFTER FOSTER CARE

There are many organizations dedicated to helping foster children make the most of their lives in ways that wouldn't be possible using only the resources of each state's child welfare system. Funds are available to pay for education, training, summer camp, and attendance at conferences where foster kids can gather together to discuss how foster care can be improved. Some of the resources you can draw on are listed here.

Casey Foundations

Members of the Casey family, the founders and heirs of United Parcel Service (UPS), have dedicated the family's foundation money to improve the lives of underprivileged children in the United States. The various foundations include the umbrella organization, Casey Family Programs; The Jim Casey Youth Opportunities Initiative; The Annie E. Casey Foundation; The Marguerite Casey Foundation; and Casey Family Services (CFS). Each foundation has a different focus.

Casey Family Programs

This is the umbrella organization, based in Seattle, established by UPS founder Jim Casey. The organization is dedicated to improving and eventually eliminating the need for foster care. The Casey website can provide links to a wide array of informative sites about funding for continuing education and is available www.casey.org/Home.

Casey Family Services

In all six New England states and in Baltimore, Maryland, this private social service agency provides additional services to children and teens in foster care. CFS actively recruits foster families, educates them about the special needs of foster children through a comprehensive training program, provides around-the-clock assistance from Casey's own case managers, therapists, and family support specialists, and offers the families additional funds to help support the foster child placed with the family.

You can apply to become a "Casey Kid" whose foster care is managed through CFS. Your foster family, your group home supervisor, or your social worker can help you get information about how to apply. If you become a Casey Kid, you will still be

(*continued*)

in your state's care, and your state caseworker will still be your legal guardian. However, Casey funding can help make it possible for you to take art classes or other lessons to maximize your talents and interests and improve your life in other ways. For more information contact www.CaseyFamily Services.org or call 203-401-6900 or 888-799-KIDS.

The Annie E. Casey Foundation

This arm of the Casey Foundations primarily awards grants to organizations whose programs will aid underprivileged children. It does not provide grants to individuals. If you know of an organization that could benefit from a Casey grant, tell them to learn more about the foundation at www.aecf.org.

The Marguerite Casey Foundation

The organization's efforts are geared toward empowering impoverished or underprivileged families and can be contacted at www.caseygrants.org.

The Jim Casey Youth Opportunities Initiative

This organization is dedicated to helping foster children transition to adulthood. As with the Annie E. Casey Foundation, in the past, grants were awarded only to organizations. However, in ten states, the Jim Casey Youth Opportunities Initiative now offers what it calls an "Opportunity Passport" to provide direct funds to kids who have been in the foster care system since age fourteen. To be eligible for the funds, young people must take a series of classes in "financial literacy." In addition, the organization directly involves young people in foster care through its system of local youth leadership boards. For more information, contact:

Jim Casey Youth Opportunities Initiative
222 South Central, Suite 305
St. Louis, MO 63105
Phone: 314-863-7000
Fax: 314-863-7003
www.jimcaseyyouth.org

National Child Welfare Resource Center for Youth Development

This organization is an adjunct of the U.S. Department of Health and Human Services and the University of Oklahoma. As one of

(*continued*)

its core principles, National Child Welfare Resource Center (NCWRC) is dedicated to youth development, which it defines as "A process which prepares young people to meet the challenges of adolescence and adulthood through a coordinated, progressive series of activities and experiences which help them to become socially, morally, emotionally, physically, and cognitively competent. Positive youth development addresses the broader developmental needs of youth, in contrast to deficit-based models which focus solely on youth problems" (from www.nrcys.ou.edu/yd/about/4core.html). It works with a National Collaboration of Youth Members to achieve its goals. For more information, see www.nrcys.ou.edu.

Daniel Memorial ("the daniel")

The daniel offers both direct and support services for youth in foster care and sponsors an annual conference for youth who are about to age out of foster care. The daniel was established as an orphanage in the 1880s and has evolved into an organization that supports services that include, but are not limited to, therapeutic foster homes for abused children, independent living services for homeless adolescents, intervention services for at-risk adolescents, and treatment for emotionally disturbed children. To learn about the daniel's programs and its conference, visit www.danielkids.org.

Connect for Kids

Connect for Kids (CFK) is a comprehensive website dedicated to informing teens in foster care about services available to them, listing and explaining contacts for kids in foster care, and providing detailed information and links about conferences for foster kids available throughout the year. You can subscribe to regular newsletters on the CFK website. When you visit www.connectforkids.org, you will know you are not alone!

worker who hasn't given you access to the tools you need for independence. Start a discussion with your social worker, and your lawyer if your state provides one, about aging out and about transitional services that are available in your state. Also, see the Sidebar on "Improve Your Life in and after Foster

Care," for tips on additional services, grants, and funding that may be available to you.

Stipends

Some states offer generous stipends for eighteen-to-twenty-two-year-olds if you apply to the child welfare office to continue in foster care through age twenty-one or twenty-two. If it's possible in your state and you decide you want to continue in your state's care, you will need to do your research and discuss your state's requirements with your social worker and your lawyer if your state provides you with one. They can help you start the application process to stay in foster care. It will be necessary to follow the steps for self-advocacy and make a good case for yourself in your application.

College

Some states will pay all the costs of college tuition and books if you continue in school, while in other states you might be granted a tuition waiver for college expenses. In some states, you will be required to attend a state (publicly funded) college or university to receive the educational subsidy. A favorite teacher or guidance counselor in your school may be a good advocate for furthering your education.

The Chafee Program

The Foster Care Independence Act (FCIA) of 1999 established the John H. Chafee Foster Care Independence Program (CFCIP), which provides federal funding for states to support young people in foster care who are aging out. The Chafee Program was designed to fund independent living programs and services for teens making the transition to adulthood. Though all states have access to Chafee Program funding and must use that funding to benefit children in foster care, each state's regulations and implementation regarding the aging-out process are slightly different.

If you could continue in your state's care after turning eighteen but think you'd rather become independent, work through your decision carefully. You may feel that you can't wait to be "free" of the state, of your social worker, or of your foster parents. Being independent could feel like a relief if foster care has been troublesome for you but giving up the state's support may not be the best thing for you in the long run.

In some states, you will not be given the choice to continue in foster care until you are twenty-one or twenty-two. You will be required to become independent on your eighteenth birthday. In most cases, you will receive neither financial aid nor support services from your state when you turn eighteen or you will receive greatly reduced financial aid and support. Some states will provide health care benefits for a limited time after you become independent.

Whatever the situation in your state, it will be important to make sure you are prepared for independence when the state no longer supports you. As stated previously, research and take advantage of all the services available to you through Chafee Program funding in your state. Your social worker and your lawyer, if you have one, can assist you in navigating the independence process, accessing Chafee Program services, and learning your rights. They can also help you learn what benefits you may have rights to after turning eighteen. Make a list of what you will need when you become independent. Be sure to include all the costs you will become responsible for once you are independent. Will you be able to earn enough money to support yourself with rent, food, transportation, clothing, and health care?

Education and Training Vouchers

One new benefit can help. Education and training vouchers (ETVs), an addition to the Chafee Independent Living Program, were federally approved in 2003 with funding to begin in October 2004. States were required to submit their plans for using the funds by June 2004, but compliance with that requirement has varied from state to state. To find out your state's plan for using ETV moneys, visit the NCWRC for youth development's website at www.nrcys.ou.edu/nrcyd/state_pages.shtml.

ETVs can be awarded "for post secondary educational and training vouchers for youth likely to experience difficulty as they transition to adulthood after the age of eighteen. This program makes available vouchers of up to $5,000 per year per youth for post secondary education and training for eligible youth." In addition, there are private funds available through the Jim Casey Youth Opportunities Initiative (www.jimcaseyyouth.org/) to ease your transition from foster care to independence.

While starting early is the best plan, if you have turned eighteen already, don't despair: The language of the Chafee Program says that its monies are designated for use by "current and former foster children aged eighteen to twenty-one." It may be more complicated to get access to those funds if you've aged out, but it is absolutely in your best interest to do your research and find out how some of that funding can help you.

WHAT YOU CAN DO AS A FOSTER CHILD

Self-Advocate

Speak up and ask for what you need and want! Learn your rights, and make sure you are receiving all the services and financial support to which you are legally entitled.

Stay in Contact with Your Social Worker

Every social worker has a card imprinted with his or her phone numbers and other contact information. Make sure you have that card and keep it in a safe place where you can always find it. Most people become social workers because they care for children and teens and want them to get the services they need and deserve. However, like all human beings, social workers aren't perfect. Most states require social workers to make a minimum number of in-person visits and calls to a foster child. However, in some states, social workers are assigned too many children's cases (this is called a *caseload*). A social worker may have to concentrate on the problem cases in the caseload, leaving little time for visits to other children.

Whether or not you are having serious problems, your social worker should be keeping track of you, taking you out of your foster home for private chats, and in general letting you know you are cared for and heard. If you are not receiving timely visits, and a lot of time goes by without a call from your social worker, speak up. Call your social worker yourself. It is your right to have a social worker to talk with.

"I will get questions from kids in foster care," about problems getting adequate information from their social worker, says attorney Violante Cote. "They'll say, 'My worker tells me that I can't go into an independent living situation until I graduate high school.' My next question [to them] will be, 'How are you going to advocate for yourself based on this information?' I will do a case scenario with them," to help identify options and ways to get in touch with their social worker. "I always tell kids involved in the case welfare system [foster care] that if they call their case worker and get no response, call again. If they call twice and get no response, call the person above them. If they still get no response, call the person above that person, until you get to a person who will respond."

In 2004, KidsCounsel wrote a booklet and produced a video for and by foster children, *I Will Speak up for Myself*, that the state makes available in a packet to all children in Connecticut's foster care program. To order copies (it costs twenty dollars), go to www.kidscounsel.org. If you believe that you need the booklet and DVD but can't afford it, call or write the KidsCounsel office at 65 Elizabeth Street Hartford, Connecticut, 06105, call at (860) 570-5327, or fax: (860) 570-5256.

Keep Track of Your School Records

If you are moved from one placement to another and the move includes changing schools, it can become difficult to maintain a record of your educational services. As you get older and prepare for high school graduation and college admission, you will need to be sure you are taking the number and type of classes you need. Your social worker is responsible for maintaining your school records. However, many young people in foster care report that social workers are overwhelmed with their caseloads and don't maintain school records reliably.

If you are being moved, do your best to get a copy of your school records from the school you are leaving, including your individualized educational program (IEP) if you have one, and a copy of your transcript, including your courses and grades. Insist that you need these records if an adult tries to tell you it isn't necessary to have them. Once you have your records, try your best to be organized about keeping them where you can find them. If you keep a three-ring binder or a file folder containing all your school papers, it will be easier to prove that you need services for your learning disabilities or that you need accommodations for physical disabilities. (See chapters 6 and 7 for more information.) If you are a good student, your transcript can help you gain admission to classes that require previous course study or to advanced placement courses.

Immediately Report Abuse

Never tolerate physical or emotional abuse from your foster family or from the staff at your group home. *Never* tolerate inappropriate sleeping arrangements, conditions that are unhealthful, whether too cold, too hot, or dirty, inadequate or poor quality food, or neglectful or irresponsible behavior. If, for example, your foster family expects or demands that you provide unpaid childcare for other children in the home, this is unacceptable. You have a right and a responsibility to yourself to file a formal complaint against your foster family if any of these abuses occur. If you believe you are unsafe in your foster home, your social worker or the court may move you to another placement on an emergency basis.

Demand Confidentiality

Confidentiality means keeping your personal business private. Your issues, including your family's past history, your own alcohol or other drug problems, your use of contraception, a pregnancy or abortion, your treatment for sexually transmitted diseases (STDs), or other personal issues can all be kept confidential by your social worker or your school. In general, most information about you is revealed to your foster family or to the staff at your group home to help them help you with your treatment plan and adjustment issues. However, there are situations in which your confidentiality can be maintained in your foster placement for your protection. Your confidentiality absolutely can and should be maintained in your community. If your confidentiality is violated, it is important to report the violation to your social worker or, if the social worker violated your confidentiality, report the violation to his or her supervisor.

Advocate for Yourself, Your Siblings, and Your Friends

Some states provide well for foster children, paying foster families an adequate stipend and offering support services that prepare the child well for reentry into their birth family, for adoption, or for independent living. Other states only do an adequate job, and some don't do well at all. For example, in 2006 the monthly stipend throughout the United States varied from two to five hundred dollars per child. As you might guess, in states that pay the lowest stipend, services provided to foster children are barely adequate. If you believe you are not being treated well by the state social services agency that oversees and pays for your care, don't keep silent. Don't be a victim. It is not your fault that you are in foster care. You deserve a good life and a successful future.

Organizations like the Youth Law Center in California (www.ylc.org) have been established to protect young people in the foster care system from abuse and neglect. The organizations will file suit against a state agency if that agency is not adequately caring for youth in foster care.

"When I was placed in foster care I thought I was the only one. I got involved in this group FFCA [Facing Foster Care in Alaska] and I was able to meet a lot of youth that were going through the same thing and it really does make a difference. We talk about everything and we have statewide meetings every three months for a weekend and it sucks that we have to leave and not see each other for another three months but we keep in contact through e-mail and calling each other. It feels really good to be close with people that are going through the same thing you are."—Kday, twenty, Alaska

Join Other Teens in Foster Care to Advocate for Better Treatment

As a foster child, you have every right to self-advocate. Speak with your friends or your siblings who are also in foster care and determine what you need to improve your situation. Organize other foster children and focus on what you need. Many states have foster youth advisory boards that bring teens like you together to discuss the issues of foster care and to advocate for themselves. If your area doesn't have a local foster youth advisory board, talk to your social worker about getting one started. Check out the Resources at the end of this chapter. Follow the steps in chapter 2. Make a plan.

There are many resources online that can help you to get organized, to learn how to improve your own situation or to get in touch with other foster kids who can help you get through a tough period in your life by sharing their experiences. One website, www.fyi3.com, is a collaboration of FosterClub.com and the Jim Casey Youth Opportunities Initiative. The website offers an opportunity for foster kids to dialogue with other foster kids. As the website said in 2006, "It's about attitudes—theirs and yours. It's about family and health care and mental health. It's about personal stories. It's about personal feelings. It's about jobs. It's about school. It's about money. It's about finding and keeping a place to live. It's about college. It's about the law. It's about rights. . . . It's about opportunities. It's free and available any time you want" (from http://www.fyi3.com/fyi3/fyi/about/index.cfm).

RESOURCES

- ABA Center on Children and the Law, Foster Care: www.abanet.org/child/fostcare.html
- National Foster Care Coalition: www.natl-fostercare.org
- Connect for Kids (part of National Foster Care Coalition): www.connectforkids.org
- Child Welfare League of America: www.cwla.org
- National Foster Parent Association: www.NFPAinc.org

- Jim Casey Youth Opportunities Initiative: www.jimcaseyyouth.org
- Casey Family Services, Annie E. Casey Foundation: www.casey.org
- Administration for Children and Families (an agency of the department of health and human services): www.acf.hhs.gov
- National Child Welfare Resource Center for Youth Development: www.nrcys.ou.edu

Bibliography

GENERAL

Administration for Children and Families, www.acf.hhs.gov.

American Bar Association Center on Children and the Law, www.abanet.org/child/home2.html.

———. "Implementation of the Foster Care Independence Act of 1999." ABA Center on Children and the Law, www.abanet.org/child/fostcare.html.

———. "National Teen Dating Violence Prevention Initiative." American Bar Association, www.abanet.org/unmet/ toolkitmaterials.html.

———. "Teen Dating Violence Awareness and Prevention Week," American Bar Association Divison for Media Relations and Communications Services, www.abavideonews.org/ABA338/index.php.

American Civil Liberties Union. ACLU Victorious in Texas Black Arm Band Case. American Civil Liberties Union, www.aclu.org/studentsrights/dresscodes/12790prs199908 30.html.

———. "Ask Sybil Liberty About Your Right to Privacy." American Civil Liberties Union, www.aclu.org/ studentsrights/privacy/12804pub19971231.html.

American Civil Liberties Union of Illinois. "Zero Tolerance." American Civil Liberties Union of Illinois, 2006,www.aclu-il.org/legal/highschool/students/ zerotolerance.shtml.

American Civil Liberties Union of New Jersey. *Students' Rights Handbook*, 2nd ed. New Brunswick: New Jersey State Bar Foundation, 2003.

American Civil Liberties Union of Northern California. "Students' Rights to Participate in Political Protest." American Civil Liberties Union of Northern California, www.aclunc.org/students/demonstrate.html.

American Immigration Law Foundation, www.ailf.org.

American Immigration Lawyers Association, www.aila.org.

Amnesty International USA. "Racial Profiling." Amnesty International USA, www.amnestyusa.org/racial_ profiling/index.do.

Assaf, Jessica. "Working for Safer Cosmetics." *New York Times Upfront*. September 18, 2006: 28.

"BAM! Body and Mind." Centers for Disease Control and Prevention, www.bam.gov.

Black, Susan. "Beyond Zero Tolerance." *American School Board Journal* 191, no. 09 (September 2004), www.asbj.com/2004/09/0904research.html.

Blake, Jeanne. *Risky Times: How to be AIDS-Smart and Stay Healthy*. New York: Workman Publishing, 1990.

"Board Of Education v. Pico 457 U.S. 853 (1982) Docket Number: 80-2043." Oyez, The U. S. Supreme Court Multimedia, www.oyez.org/oyez/resource/case/1060.

Boston College Law School, www.bc.edu/schools/law.

Bova, Carla. "Local Teens See Bill Signed into Law." *Marin Independent Journal* (October 11, 2005), www.breastcancerfund.org/site/apps/nl/content3 .asp?c=kwKXLdPaE&b=86382&ct=1500019.

"*Brown v. Board of Education*, 347 U.S. 483 (1954) (USSC+)." Supreme Court of the United States, www.nationalcenter .org/brown.html.

Canalori, Richard. "Debating Teenage Rights." Yale–New Haven Teachers Institute (2005), www.yale.edu/ynhti/ curriculum/units/1988/1/88.01.01.x.html.

Casey Family Programs. "Casey Family Programs Provides and Improves—and Ultimately Prevents the Need For—Foster Care." Casey Family Programs, www.casey.org.

Center for Children's Advocacy Publications and Videos, www.kidscounsel.org/aboutus_publications.htm.

———. *I Will Speak Up for Myself*. Video, Hartford, Conn., Center for Children's Advocacy, Inc. 2004.

———. "Teen Legal Advocacy Clinic." University of Connecticut School of Law. Center for Children's Advocacy, www.kidscounsel.org/aboutus_programs_tlac .htm.

Child Welfare League of America, www.cwla.org.

Children's Law Center, www.childrenslawcenter.org.

Children's Law Center of Massachusetts Inc., www.clcm.org.

Connect for Kids (part of National Foster Care Coalition), www.connectforkids.org.

Cortiella, Candace. "IDEA 2004 Close Up: Transition Planning." Charles and Helen Schwab Foundation, www.schwablearning.org/articles.asp?r=998.

Curtis, Paul C. "Legal Options Offered to Teen Parents." *The Garden Island* (March 28, 2006) www.kauaiworld.com/ articles/2006/02/28/news/news04.txt.

Dawson, Dr. Jody. "Self Advocacy: A Valuable Skill for Your Teenager." Charles and Helen Schwab Foundation, www.schwablearning.org/articles.asp?r=522&g=2.

Disability Rights Education and Defense Fund. "Access Equals Opportunity." Disability Rights Education and Defense Fund, www.dredf.org/technical_assistance/forward.shtml.

Dowling-Sendor, Benjamin. "Balancing Safety with Free Expression." *American School Board Journal* 188, no. 12 (December 2001), www.asbj.com/2001/12/ 1201schoollaw.html.

———. "Discipline on the Road." *American School Board Journal* (February 2000), www.asbj.com/2000/02/ 0200schoollaw.html.

———. "The Due Process Clause and Corporal Punishment." *American School Board Journal* 188, no. 4 (April 2001), www.asbj.com/2001/04/0401schoollaw.html.

———. "A Matter of Disruption, not Dress." *American School Board Journal* (August 1998), www.asbj.com/ 199808/0898schoollaw.html.

———. "A Question of Rights vs. Authority." *American School Board Journal* 188, no. 7 (July 2001), www.asbj.com/2001/07/0701schoollaw.html.

———. "A Search for the Right Answer" *American School Board Journal* 189, no. 1 (January 2002), www.asbj.com/2002/01/0102schoollaw.html.

———. "What Not to Wear" *American School Board Journal* 192, no. 8 (August 2005), www.asbj.com/2005/08/0805schoollaw.html.

Ethnic Majority. "Racial Profiling of African, Hispanic (Latino), and Asian Americans." Ethnic Majority, www.ethnicmajority.com/racial_profiling.htm.

Fernandez, Happy Craven. *The Child Advocacy Handbook*. New York: The Pilgrim Press, 1980.

Firschein, Merry. "Student Wins Right to Skirt Rules." *The Bergen County Record*, January 25, 2006: A-1, 14.

Fisher, Roger, William Ury, and Bruce Patton. *Getting to YES*. Boston: Houghton Mifflin, 1981.

———. "Global Negotiation Project." Harvard University, www.pon.harvard.edu/research/projects/gnp.php3.

Fortas, Justice Abe, "Opinion of the Court, *Tinker et al. v. Des Moines, Independent Community School District et al.*" No. 21 Supreme Court of the United States, 393 U.S. 503. Argued November 12, 1968, Decided February 24, 1969, www.bc.edu/bc_org/avp/cas/comm/free_speech/tinker.html.

Gay, Lesbian and Straight Education Network, www.glsen.org/cgi-bin/iowa/all/home.html.

Gender.Org. "Welcome to Gender.Org." Gender.org, www.gender.org/index.html.

Gibb, Sarah, ed. *The Advocacy Manual for Sexuality Education, Health and Justice: Resources for Communities of Faith*. Boston: Unitarian Universalist Association, 1999.

"Goss v. Lopez 419 U.S. 565 (1975) Docket Number: 73-898." Oyez, The U. S. Supreme Court Multimedia, www.oyez.org/oyez/resource/case/146.

"*Gratz v. Bollinger*, 539 U.S. 244 (2003) Docket Number: 02-516." Oyez, The U. S. Supreme Court, Multimedia, at www.oyez.org/oyez/resource/case/1540/.

Gregory, Daphne, "S-4, Student Self-Survival Skills Project." College of Education at University of Illinois, Urbana, www.ed.uiuc.edu/sped/tri/studentselfsurvival.htm.

Halstead, Richard. "Students take their cosmetics case to the state capital." *Marin Independent Journal* (September 20, 2005), www.breastcancerfund.org/site/apps/nl/content3.asp?c=kwKXLdPaE&b=85314&ct=1439739.

Hudson, David L., Jr. *The Silencing of Student Voices: Preserving Free Speech in America's Schools.* 2003 First Amendment Center, www.firstamendmentcenter.org/PDF/Silencing.intro.pdf#search=%22jennifer%20boccia%22.

Human Rights Educational Associates. "Human Rights Day, (10 December 2006)." Human Rights Educational Associates, www.hrea.org/feature-events/human-rights-day.php.

"In re Gault, 387 U.S. 1 (1967) Docket Number: 116." Oyez, The U.S. Supreme Court Multimedia, at www.oyez.org/oyez/resource/case/181.

Janofsky, Michael. "Gay Rights Battlefields Spread to Public Schools," *New York Times*, June 9, 2005: A-18.

Jim Casey Youth Opportunities Initiative, www.jimcaseyyouth.org.

Johnson, John W. *The Struggle for Student Rights: Tinker v. Des Moines and The 1960s.* Lawrence: University of Kansas Press, 1997; reviewed at *The Law and Politics Book Review*, www.unt.edu/lpbr/subpages/newrevs/johnsj98.htm.

Johnson, Nancy S. J. "Self Advocacy: Know Yourself, Know What You Need, Know How to Get It." Peter W. D. Wright and Pamela Darr Wright at Wrightslaw, www.wrightslaw.com/info/sec504.selfadvo.ld.johnson.htm.

Julianelle, Patricia F. "Educating Homeless Students under the Reauthorized McKinney-Vento Act." National School Boards Association, www.nsba.org/site/doc_cosa.asp?TRACKID=&DID=33536&CID=164.

Kids as Self Advocates. "Our Theory of Change." Kids as Self Advocates, www.fvkasa.org/theory.html.

Killeen, Wendy. "Preventing Teen Violence." *Boston Globe.* July 13, 2006: *Globe North* 7.

King, Dr. Martin Luther, Jr., "Letter from Birmingham Jail." In *Why We Can't Wait*, ed. Martin Luther King Jr. New York: Signet Paperbacks, 1964.

Krebs, Betsy, and Paul Pitcoff. *On Your Own as a Young Adult*. Indianapolis, Ind.: JIST Publishing, 2006.

Leuchovius, Deborah. "Parent Advocacy Coalition for Educational Rights." ADA Q & A: Section 504 & Postsecondary Education 1994, www.pacer.org/text/pride/504.htm.

Lewis, Diane E. "Bill Aims to Upgrade Child Labor Laws." *Boston Globe*. July 20, 2006: D5.

MacFarquhar, Neil. "A Simple Scarf, But Meaning Much More Than Faith." *New York Times*. September 8, 2006: A22.

Massachusetts Coalition for Occupational Safety Health's, www.masscosh.org.

Merriam-Webster's Collegiate Dictionary, 10th ed. Springfield, Mass: Merriam-Webster, Incorporated, 1993: 18.

Meyer Foundation. "DC's Young Women Work to Change the System." The Meyer Foundation, www.meyerfoundation.org/greatideas/greatideas_show.htm?doc_id=251284.

National Center for Learning Disabilities. "Being Your Own Advocate." National Center for Learning Disabilities, www.ncld.org/index.php?option=content&task=view&id=481.

National Center for Missing and Exploited Children, www.missingkids.com.

National Center for Youth Law, www.youthlaw.org/myrights.htm.

National Coalition to Support Sexuality Education, www.ncsse.org/mandates.html.

National Council for Occupational Safety and Health, www.coshnetwork.org.

National Drug Safety Network. "Congress Proposes Drug Testing all High School Students." National Drug Strategy Network, www.ndsn.org/summer99/test1.html.

National Foster Care Coalition, www.natl-fostercare.org.

National Foster Parent Association, www.NFPAinc.org.

National Resource Center for Youth Services, www.nrcys.ou
.edu.

National Youth Advocacy Coalition, www.nyacyouth.org/nyac/
about.html.

New York Civil Liberties Union. "Information on Students'
Civil Rights re: Sexuality." New York Civil Liberties
Union, www.nyclu.org.

New York State Education Department. "Student Advocacy
Handbook for High School Juniors and Seniors
Transitioning to College." New York State Education
Department, Vocational and Educational Services for
Individuals with Disabilities, www.vesid.nysed.gov/
specialed/transition/sah1.html.

Nolo.com. "Your Rights against Discrimination Based on
Sexual Orientation." Nolo.com, www.nolo.com/article
.cfm/ObjectID/0F606661-EF27-4560-
9191693C7FFA61B3/catID/57153B2E-F39E-48DA-
830ADA31F5A23325/104/150/175/ART/.

O'Rourke, Rhian Kohashi. "Becoming Sex Ed Girl." Campus
Progress, www.campusprogress.org/soundvision/236/
becoming-sex-ed-girl.

"Regents of the University of California v. Bakke, 438 U.S. 265
(1978) Docket Number: 76-811." Oyez, The U. S.
Supreme Court, Multimedia, www.oyez.org/oyez/
resource/case/324.

Santos, Fernanda. "Protest over Metal Detectors Gains Legs,
Students Walk Out." *New York Times*. September 21,
2005: B1, B4

Serve Center. McKinney-Vento, National Center for Homeless
Education, www.serve.org/nche/m-v.php.

Sex, Etc. "Why Wonder?" Sex, Etc., www.sexetc.org/index.php.

SIECUS Community. "Community Action Kit." SIECUS
Community, www.communityactionkit.org.

Silva, JoAnn Augeri. *Media Training Guidelines*. Marblehead,
Mass.: Lexicon Communicating, 1999–2006.

Spacks, Patricia Meyer, ed. *Advocacy in the Classroom, Problems
and Possibilities*. New York: St. Martin's Press, 1996.

Stone, Martha. *I Will Speak Up for Myself: Your Legal Rights in Foster Care.* Hartford, Conn.: Center for Children's Advocacy, Inc., 2004.

Substance Abuse and Mental Health Services Administration. "Drug Facts." Substance Abuse and Mental Health Services Administration, Family Guide: Keeping Youth Mentally Healthy and Drug Free, www.family.samhsa.gov/main/facts.aspx.

——. "Peer Pressure: Good or Bad?" Substance Abuse and Mental Health Services Administration, Family Guide: Keeping Youth Mentally Healthy and Drug Free, www.family.samhsa.gov/teach/ppressure.aspx.

Transition Matters—From School to Independence. New York, N.Y.: Resources for Children with Special Needs, 2003.

Triano, Sarah. "Disabled and Proud," www.disabledandproud.com/power.htm.

United Nations. "Universal Declaration of Human Rights." United Nationals General Assembly, Adopted and proclaimed by General Assembly resolution 217 A (III) of 10 December 1948, at www.un.org/Overview/rights.html.

U.S. Department of Education. "Sexual Harassment Guidance." U.S. Department of Education, www.ed.gov/print/about/offices/list/ocr/docs/sexhar01.html.

U.S. Department of Health and Human Services. "Alcohol Alert." U.S. Department of Health and Human Services, pubs.niaaa.nih.gov/publications/AA67/AA67.pdf.

——. "Your Rights under Section 504 of the Rehabilitation Act." U.S. Department of Health and Human Services, Office of Civil Rights, at www.hhs.gov/ocr/504.html.

U.S. Department of Housing and Urban Development, www.hud.gov.

U.S. Department of Justice. "A Guide to Disability Rights Law." U. S. Department of Justice, Civil Rights Division, www.usdoj.gov/crt/ada/cguide.htm.

U.S. Department of Labor. "Child Labor Introduction." U. S. Department of Labor, www.dol.gov/elaws/esa/flsa/cl/default.htm.

———. "Employment Rights Who Has Them and Who Enforces Them." U.S. Department of Labor, www.dol.gov/odep/pubs/fact/rights.htm.

U.S. Equal Opportunity Employment Commission. "EEOC Releases ADA Policy Guidance on Job Accommodations for Individuals with Disabilities." U. S. Equal Opportunity Employment Commission, www.eeoc.gov/press/3-1-99.html.

———. "The Civil Rights Act of 1991." U.S. Equal Employment Opportunity Commission, www.eeoc.gov/policy/cra91.html.

———. "Filing a Charge of Employment Discrimination." U.S. Equal Opportunity Employment Commission, www.eeoc.gov/charge/overview_charge_filing.html.

Walls, David. *Activist's Almanac: The Concerned Citizen's Guide to the Leading Advocacy Organizations in America*. New York: Fireside, Simon & Schuster, 1993.

Welfare Research, Inc. *Handbook for Youth in Foster Care*. Albany: New York State Office of Children and Family Services, 2004.

Wilson, Pamela M. *Our Whole Lives: Sexuality Education for Grades 7–9*. Boston: Unitarian Universalist Association, 1999.

Wright, Peter W.D. "The Individuals with Disabilities Education Improvement Act of 2004," Wrightslaw.com, www.wrightslaw.com/idea/idea.2004.all.pdf.

Youth Alive. *Teens on Target, Advocacy Manual*, A Project of Youth Alive, www.youthalive.org/Advocacy_Manual.pdf.

Young Women's Project, www.youngwomensproject.org.

Index

About the Authors

Cheryl Gerson Tuttle has more than thirty years experience in education, counseling, and advocacy. She is the coauthor of five books including *Learning Disabilities: The Ultimate Teen Guide* (2003) and the author of *Medications: The Ultimate Teen Guide* (2005). She is the mother of two sons and the grandmother of three.

JoAnn Augeri Silva is an award-winning writer, editor, public relations professional, and journalism teacher whose work has appeared in numerous publications. She is a cum laude graduate of the University of Connecticut. She is an experienced media coach, a certified sexuality education teacher, and a former foster parent. She is the mother of an adult son and daughter and the grandmother of three.